# Our Great War Heroes: Six Param Vir Chakra Recipients

## Volume 2

# Our Great War Heroes: Six Param Vir Chakra Recipients

## Volume 2

(True Stories of Six Flaming Warriors of Indian Army)

*Shyam Kumari*

**Vij Books India Pvt Ltd**

**New Delhi (India)**

*Published by*

**Vij Books India Pvt Ltd**
(Publishers, Distributors & Importers)
2/19, Ansari Road
Delhi – 110 002
Phones: 91-11-43596460, 91-11-47340674
M: 98110 94883
e-mail: contact@vijpublishing.com
web: www.vijbooks.in



ISBN: 978-93-90439-73-7 (Hardback)
ISBN: 978-93-90439-78-2 (Paperback)
ISBN: 978-93-90439-05-8 (ebook)

## Also by Shyam Kumari

### *English:*

Vignettes of Sri Aurobindo and the Mother

More Vignettes of Sri Aurobindo and the Mother

Beautiful Vignettes of Sri Aurobindo and the Mother

How They Came to Sri Aurobindo and the Mother, Volumes 1 to 4

Musings on the Mother's Prayers and Meditations, Volumes 1 to 3

Sunlit Days

Sweet Steps

Towards Light

Teacher's Guide to Sunlit Days, Sweet Steps and Towards Light

Lights from Nolini Kanta Gupta (compilation)

### *Hindi:*

Bharat, Vishwa aur Manavta ka Bhavishya – Sri Aravind evam Sri Ma kay Alok may

Bhagwan Ki Oar, Parts 1 and 2

Sri Arvind Aur Sri Ma Ki Divya Lila, Parts 1 and 2

Gulab Ki Pankhuriyan (21 stories)

Aparajita (24 stories and 2 plays)

Prem Divani (35 stories and 2 plays)

Jeenay Ki Kala, Parts 1 and 2

Anupam Kahaniya Arambhik, Part 1

Anupam Kahaniya, Parts 1 to 4

Madhur Kahaniya, Parts 1 and 2

Shishu Rang Tarang, Part 1

Nav Bal Rang Tarang, Parts 1 and 2

Nav Rag Anurag

Shri Arvind Sahitya – Jyotirmaya Tarange

The following books are available both in English and Hindi:

Our Great Revolutionaries (1): Chandrashekhar 'Azad'

Our Great Revolutionaries (2): Kanailal Dutt

Param Vir Chakra Recipients (1): Major Som Nath Sharma

Param Vir Chakra Recipients (5): Second Lieutenant Rama Raghoba Rane

Param Vir Chakra Recipients (8): Major Shaitan Singh

Param Vir Chakra Recipients (9): Colonel Dhan Singh Thapa

Param Vir Chakra Recipients (10): Coy Quartermaster Havildar Abdul Hamid

Param Vir Chakra Recipients (11): Lt. Col. Ardeshir Burzorji Tarapore

Param Vir Chakra Recipients (12): Lance Naik Albert Ekka

Param Vir Chakra Recipients (13): Second Lieutenant Arun Khetarpal

Param Vir Chakra Recipients (16): Hon. Captain Bana Singh

Param Vir Chakra Recipients (18): Captain Vikram Batra

Param Vir Chakra Recipients (19): Captain Manoj Kumar Pandey

Param Vir Chakra Recipients (20): Grenadier Yogender Singh Yadav

Param Vir Chakra Recipients (21): Rifleman Sanjay Kumar

# Contents

# Dedication

**I dedicate this book at the lotus feet of Sri Aurobindo**

who renounced all personal comforts and bore unimaginable hardships for India,

who declared in unambiguous words that India was a "Godhead" and the "Mother",

who, by his mantric words, infused a new life in the youth of the almost dead and depressed nation, through his journals "Bande Mataram" and "Karmayogin",

who, while imprisoned in the Alipore Jail by the British, had the realisation of "Vasudev",

who was foremost amongst the revolutionaries and shook the throne of the British Empire by his yogashakti.

**And also at the lotus feet of the Mother**

who, unbeknown to the world, is guarding India

and leading the whole Creation towards a golden future.

# Acknowledgements

Many persons have helped with their inputs and encouragement in the making of this book. One day during a phone conversation, my friend Maj. Gen. Mrinal Suman mentioned that the families of two PVCs, Second Lieutenant Rama Raghoba Rane and Major Dhan Singh Thapa live in Pune. He emailed me their addresses and phone numbers. In August 2012, a Mumbai-based patriot-friend Shri Rakesh Oza went to Pune thrice to interview the two families. The wives and children of PVCs Rane and Thapa were delighted and touched by this unexpected turn of the events. They were gratified that at a time when everybody in India, except the military, seemed to have forgotten the PVCs, somebody remembers them and wants to write and publish their stories. I am grateful to Mrs. Rajeshwari Rane who gave Shri Rakesh Oza intimate and invaluable information about some hitherto unknown incidents of PVC Second Lieutenant Rama Raghoba Rane's life. In addition PVC Rane's regiment, Bombay Engineers' Group's write up, has supplied me many facts about PVC Rama Ragobha Rane's life-story. Shri Rakesh Oza interviewed PVC Major Dhan Singh Thapa's wife, Mrs. Shukla Thapa and her daughter, Poornima Thapa as well. He e-mailed me some authentic facts about his life. Later Miss Poornima Thapa sent a detailed account of her illustrious father's story. Whenever I asked for any additional information she promptly supplied it. She also sent me the reminiscences of Col. A.S. Sharma. I sincerely thank Mrs Shukla Thapa and Miss Poornima Thapa. For writing the story of PVC Major Shaitan Singh, Shri Rakesh Oza, went to Falodi (now called Major Shaitan Singh Nagar) to interview Shri Narpat Singh, the only son of PVC Major Shaitan Singh, with a view to collect some personal glimpses from his early life. Shri Narpat Singh presented him a book *Smriti Granth Rastraveer Major Shaitan Singh*. From this book I got the invaluable last letters written by our Hero to his friend

Shaurya Chakra winner Col. Malsingh and to his brother-in-law, Mool Singh Ji, as well as the tributes of Narayan Singh Bhati and the reminiscences of his close friend, Col. Malsingh and Narayan Singh Bhati. I sincerely thank Shri Narpat Singh.

To write the story of PVC Abdul Hamid, I contacted his second son, Shri Ali Hasan, who kindly gave me many facts about his hero father's life before he joined the Army, as well as many relevant facts about his Army life. He also sent details about his father's legacy; memorials, stamps released in his name and the honours bestowed upon him. I also had a telephone conversation with the PVC's widow, Mrs. Rasoolan Bibi. The indefatigable Rakesh Oza went to Kanpur and interviewed Shri Ali Hasan. I sincerely thank Shri Ali Hasan and Mrs Rasoolan Bibi and Shri Rakesh Oza.

In January 2008 when PVCs Sanjay Kumar and Yogender Singh came to Delhi to lead the 26th January Republic Day parade, my niece, Miss Taru, invited them to her house and my sister, Raka and her husband Shri Satya Prakash, interviewed both the PVCs on my behalf. Dear Raka transcribed the taped interviews and sent the script to me. I thank Raka and Shri Satya Prakash, who have constantly supported me in this noble endeavour. Upon my request, PVC Sanjay Kumar also wrote his story and posted it to me. Later he corrected the final typescript. My sincere thanks to PVC Sanjay Kumar.

I was worried whom to send to Jari, a remote Adivasi village of Jharkhand, to interview the family of PVC Albert Ekka. Lt. Col. Samrat Nagar of 14 Guards deputed a dynamic patriot, retired Maj. Devendra Nath Das of 14 Guards, who made a 530-miles trip to Jari, with two videographers and some friends in two vehicles and interviewed the family and friends of PVC Albert Ekka and helped me talk on the phone with Mrs. Balamdina, the venerable widow of PVC Albert Ekka. Maj. Devendra Nath Das also sent me photocopies of the Regimental papers, his own detailed reminiscences, photographs and cuttings from old newspapers about PVC Albert Ekka. I thank Lt. Col. Samrat Nagar and Maj. Devendra Nath Das with all my heart.

I also thank the following for their help and support: (Late) Maj. Gen. K. K. Tewari PVSM, AVSM; Lt. Gen. (Retd.) Jagdish Chander

PVSM, AVSM, VSM, ADC; Maj. Gen. (Retd.) Ian Cardozo; Maj. Gen. (Retd.) Mrinal Suman, AVSM, VSM, PhD; Maj. Gen. (Retd.) Raj Mehta; Maj. Gen. (Retd.) Suresh K. Thadani; Maj. Gen. (Retd.) G. S. Bal VSM General Officer Commanding, 36 Infantry Division; Colonel (Retd.) Lalit Kumar Rai, VRC; Colonel MahipTomar; Dr. Larry Siedlitz; Dr. N.K. Kalia; Shri Arun Churiwal; Shri Shankar Poddar, Shri O.P. Dani, Shri Satish Deora; Ms Maria Jain and Ms Vilas Patel.

I am grateful to Brig. P. K. Vij of Vij Publishing Group for bringing out this book.

Most of all, I thank my son Kim for his constant support.

Listed below are sources of information which have helped me write this book:

- Claude Arpi, author of 'Braving the Heights' in *The Pioneer*, 28 February 2007.
- Maj. Gen. (Retd.) Ian Cardozo, author of *Param Vir - Our Heroes in Battle.*
- (Late) Maj. Gen. K. K. Tewari, PVSM, AVSM, author of *A Soldier's Voyage of Self-Discovery.*
- Lt. Gen. Dr. M. L. Chibber PVSM, AVSM, PhD (Retd.) author of *Pakistan's Criminal Folly in Kashmir.*
- Lieutenant Colonel Rajkumar Pattu and Brigadier Man Mohan Sharma, authors of *Indian Prisoners of War in Pakistan.*
- Brigadier L.P. Sen, author of *Slender Was the Thread.*
- Lieutenant Colonel A. Asthana, Commanding Officer 1/11 Gorkha Rifles.
- T. Samphel, author of *Unsung Heroes of Kargil War.*
- Srinjoy Chowdhury, author of *Despatches from Kargil.*
- Gaurav Savant, author of *Dateline Kargil.*

- Amar Nath Saraf, author of *Rajouri Remembered.*
- Maj. Gen. L.S. Lehl's article 'A Nation Divided and the 1947 Indo-Pak War' published in the book *The Indian Army, a Brief History.*
- Sushree Rachana Bisht Rawat, author of *The Brave.*
- *Smriti Granth Rastraveer Major Shaitan Singh.*

Search Engines - Internet:

- 'Heroism' - Bharat Rakshak.
- 'The Indian behind the Param Vir Chakra' - google.com.

## Foreword By

## (Late) Maj. Gen. K. K. Tewari, PVSM, AVSM

I consider it a privilege to be asked to write a 'Foreword' to this series on 'Our Heroes'. This series of books on modern Indian Heroes serves an important and long overdue need. Stories of valour and heroism can awaken a spirit of emulation in others. There is nothing more precious than life. And yet, a soldier in the country's service may be called upon to offer this most precious of all things as if it were a mere trifle.

In five decades since India's Independence, the Indian soldier has repeatedly made the supreme sacrifice. India owes an immeasurable debt to the untold thousands of soldiers who have died uncelebrated in her service. The 21 recipients of the Param Vir Chakra are the few acknowledged symbols of the unknown soldiers and their many exceptional acts of courage and sacrifice.

A wilful act of self sacrifice performed as an act of duty can only come from a tremendous training in character. What high training engenders the fortitude and bravery which converts ordinary boys, and increasingly now, girls into selfless heroes? Were it possible to adapt this training in character and bravery to the needs of civil life, India would be an extremely effective society. The need of the hour is to find the methods and means to generalise this capacity for heroism, routinely demonstrated by soldiers defending India's borders, into the youth of India who constitute the largest segment of India's population and are the hope of her future.

The author Shyam Kumari of Sri Aurobindo Ashram deserves to be complimented on this laudable project she has undertaken. The political leadership and the academicians in the country would do well to introduce such stories of gallantry in the service of the nation in all schools, colleges and other training institutions of the country.

Sri Aurobindo has described the need for awakening a spirit in the service of the nation in an article titled "The Bourgeois and the Samurai" written in the early 20th century while comparing India and Japan, which should be read by all thinking Indians.

# Farewell to a Martyr

Speak not, speed not
O traveller! Softly pass
On this flower-strewn road,
For here in repose,
On his way to an eternal abode,
Lies the body of a young martyr,
Ready for the funeral pyre.
Thick is the jasmine odour,
Red the flame
Of burning camphor,
Plaintive the notes
Of the bard's sad lyre
As he sings the tale
Of heroic valour
Of this son of India
Who traversed a way
Most arduous.
In a grief-warp,
The frail mother is caught

From a pain so sharp,—
O how can solace be sought?
From her stunned heart
Escapes no sigh,
As she clings to him
Who was her life.
Whose eyes were
Two lamps of light.
The mother devastated,
A monument of sorrow
Pleads with death,
Alas, in vain,
To let her borrow
Just one moment
Of her son's brief life,
O, let him speak
Some loving last words
To his broken mother,
His shattered father,
His bereft sister,
His stunned brothers.
Ah, this sweet boy
She suckled,

A toddler, in her arms who nestled,
With loving care, whom she nurtured:
Her brave son, so intensely loved.
Wife stunned, her heart riven torn as under.
Hopes dead, future bleak,
Day her enemy, night a torture.
Child forlorn, orphaned, bewildered.
For the journey's last leg
On the gun-carriage
His body draped in a flag
They reverently lay.
How cruel this march
How cruel this way
Their feet traverse
As their arms they reverse
The bugles' plaintive notes
To the heavens form an arch.
The father tries to hold back
His spilling tears
Proud of his son
As he sets alight the pyre.
In state after state
In cities and villages

Across the land of India
Thousands keep vigil,
As burn radiant with valour's
Eternal light
The mortal remains
Of India's martyrs.
Proud is Mother India
Of its worthy sons,
Of them she will not
Forget one.
Vain is not their sacrifice,
Vain is not the snuffing
Of their precious lives.
Their great deeds
Will steel and light
Our hearts and minds
Calling us to play our parts
As well, to die willingly
In India's defence,
To win at whatever cost
Mother India's battles.

# Preface

For a nation to preserve its Independence and protect itself against foreign domination, it is imperative that it awakens the spirit of bravery and establishes the ideal of the Kshatriya in the hearts of its citizens.

At a particular epoch of Indian history, due to the influence of the Buddhist doctrine of the unreality of life and the theory of Mayavad or Illusionism, India lost her strength. Indians forgot the ideals of bravery as embodied by her ancient heroes, Lord Ram, Lord Krishna, Arjuna and Bhima, to name only a few. Due to an excessive stress on the life beyond, the Life-Instinct in the Indians dwindled. The number of warriors and soldiers decreased, while those of Sannyasins and mendicants increased. It is said that at one time in Bihar alone there were nine lakh monasteries.

Belief in the unreality of life caused India to lose her grip on the outer world. As a result, foreign invaders and barbarians marched into India and looted and crushed the country repeatedly. Lakhs of Indians were butchered and millions were forcibly converted to the religion of the invaders. The matchless bravery of India seemed lost. For centuries India remained a slave nation, exploited by different conquerors. Indians lost the right to walk with their heads held high; worse still, the nation lost its self-confidence and self-respect.

After centuries of torpor, the spirit of nationalism awoke in the 19th century. The real battle for freedom of the country began in 1857 with the sacrifice of Queen Lakshmi Bai of Jhansi. Thousands of freedom fighters and countless soldiers died in the battle of liberation or languished in British jails for decades. They bore the terrible atrocities of the Cellular Jail in the Andamans and fearlessly faced the batons, bayonets and bullets of the British police and the British

Army. Many were killed or exiled. As a result of the sacrifice of these martyrs the great day of 15th August 1947 dawned, the chains of slavery were severed, India regained her freedom and once again we could hold our heads high.

Unfortunately, we seemed to forget the story of the subjection of our country. On the one hand, for decades the political arena became a dark field where the lowest universal forces became active. On the other hand, forgetting the shameful centuries of slavery, forgetting the sacrifice of those who gave their lives so that the country might gain freedom, we became enamoured of wealth and comfort. Our young men receive very high, almost undreamed of, salaries from multinational corporations while, sadly, the Indian Army is short of thousands of officers. Though with the advent of Shri Narendra Modi India has taken a patriotic orientation. The sacred slogans of "Bharatmata Ki Jai" and "Vande Mataram" are being chanted by millions of Indians again.

Today India is surrounded by hostile neighbours. China and Pakistan seem to have become our eternal enemies. From Tibet, scores of China's nuclear missiles are targeted towards India. In the present circumstances, no weak nation can hope to remain safe. Powerful nations can crush any weak nation. If India becomes weak, she can be dominated and conquered by other powers.

To safeguard her Independence, India needs to keep the flame of nationalism and bravery burning brightly in the hearts of her children. To kindle the flame of self-sacrifice, it is necessary to imprint in the hearts of the youth the stories of our revolutionary heroes who suffered terrible atrocities and even climbed the gallows with a smile and the cry "Bharatmata Ki Jai" on their lips. Also, we should tell them the stories of our brave soldiers and officers who have sacrificed their lives in the defence of the country after Independence.

We have to imprint in the hearts of each child, teenager and youth of the nation the sacred life stories of our martyrs. If this is done, the spirit of the Kshatriya will reawaken in the children of India. They will become burning flames of nationalism. They will compete to be the first to sacrifice his life for the country. Then, no nation, however powerful, will dare to invade India. An independent India, a great India, will establish the rule of Truth in the world, and will fulfil the prophecy of Sri Aurobindo by becoming the guru of the world.

The Divine Mother of Sri Aurobindo Ashram had always supported the Indian Army. Once she had said, ". . . Army is the only hope for India."

Lord Wavell had predicated the survival of India as one entity on the preservation of the Indian Army as an effective and irreproachable instrument.

Below I quote from a prayer written by Sri Aurobindo, which I hope will become the constant prayer of numerous children of Mother India:

"Mother Durga! India lies low in selfishness and fearfulness and littleness. Make us great, make our efforts great, our hearts vast, make us true to our resolve. May we no longer desire the small, void of energy, given to laziness, stricken with fear."

With humble Pranams to Sri Aurobindo and the Mother.

Shyam Kumari

Sri Aurobindo Ashram, Pondicherry

# Second Lieutenant Rama Raghoba Rane

## Birth and Childhood

During the Mugal rule in Northern India, many Rajput nobles migrated to South India and founded small principalities. One of these groups settled in Goa. So fiery and fearless were these brave Rajputs that for fifty years they fought the Portuguese bitterly. One of these courageous nobles was an ancestor of Second Lieutenant Rama Raghoba Rane, who had settled in a small village of Chendia in the North Kanara District of Bombay. Our hero Rama Ragobha Rane was the second son from amongst the eight children of Shri Raghoba Rane and Srimati Gopica Rane. He was born on 26 June 1918 in Kukallim village of Goa. He had four brothers and three sisters.

## *Athiti Devo Bhava*: The Guest is God

Raghoba Rane and Gopica Rane had an ardent and living faith in God. Their children imbibed the faith of their parents. Child Rama also had deep faith in God. An intensely religious family, the Ranes not only believed in but also lived the ideals as inscribed in the scriptures for householders. They treated a guest as a god: *Athiti Devo Bhava*. They also instilled these ideals in their children. If some guest chanced to come when there was little food in the house, child Rama would pretend that he was not hungry and ask his mother to give his share to the guest.

## Early Education

Since Rama's head constable father was transferred from place to place, his early education took place in different district schools. From his childhood Rama showed a keen interest in sports and extra-curricular activities such as scouting. He passed his S.S.C. examination from Karwar.

***Family Picture***

## Patriotic Fervour: Non-Cooperation Movement

Rama Raghoba Rane was a born patriot. Even before entering his teens he began to take interest in the Non-Cooperation Movement against the British which began in 1930 and helped the Satyagrahis

(Indians fighting against the British). His father was alarmed. Being a constable in the state police, he did not want his son to become a Satyagrahi, therefore he shifted his family to his native village Chendia. Thus ended our hero Rama's brave urge to participate in the freedom movement.

## Joins the Army

In 1940 the Second World War was in full swing. The changing scenario of the terrible War from day to day, with armies marching, armies victorious and armies defeated, gripped the consciousness of humanity. Adventurous by nature 22 year old Rama Rane decided to join the Army. On 10 July 1940 he enrolled in the Bombay Engineers.

### Best Recruit: Win's Commandant's Cane: Promoted as Naik

Rama Rane was adjudged the best recruit in his batch and was presented with the Commandant's Cane and was promoted to the rank of Naik.

## Naik Rama Raghoba In Burma

After completing his training Naik Rama Raghoba was posted to the 28 Field Company which, working under 26 Infantry Division, was fighting the Japanese in the jungles of Burma. Once on the Buthidaung front the entire 26 Infantry Division had to retreat. The Commander left two sections of 28 Field Company under Naik Rama Raghoba to destroy ammunition dumps and many Army vehicles which had to be left behind, to save them from falling in the hands of the Japanese. Even though the Japanese were advancing and surrounding them, Rane and his men fulfilled their task. After the completion of the destruction work, these sections were supposed to be picked up by the navy. However, the navy craft could not come to their rescue because the enemy was very close. The Japanese surrounded the destruction squad. The situation seemed hopeless for the trapped men of these two sections.

### Successful Retreat Across the River: Promoted to Havildar

It is in such situations that the exceptional warrior makes a way where there seems none. The Japanese were watching and intensely patrolling the river. Naik Rama Raghoba eluded the enemy for four days. He with his men escaped in a boat. The boat leaked badly and began to fill with water. With great presence of mind Naik Rama Raghoba plugged the leaks with sacks of flour and brought back his troops safely. The two sections joined their Division at Bahri Bazar. For this brave feat Rama Raghoba was promoted to the rank of Havildar.

## The 1947-48 Indo-Pakistan War: Promoted to Second Lieutenant

Promotions came swiftly to Rama Raghoba Rane. He was first made a Naik, then a Havildar and in 1947, when the country gained independence, he was selected for a commission as Second Lieutenant.

For Second Lieutenant Rama Raghoba Rane the moment of glory, of winning India's highest medal for bravery, the Param Vir Chakra, was nearing. But before we move to that moment of unimaginable bravery let us throw back a glance at the political scenario at the time of 1947-48 Indo-Pakistan War.

### 1947: Kashmir Attacked – Thousands Perish

Here it is necessary to glance at the sequence of events which led to the 1947-48 War between India and Pakistan. In 1947 our Mother India had been partitioned in two. A new country Pakistan was carved with some Muslim majority provinces. The more than 500 princely states were given the option of joining either country. There were terrible riots in which millions were killed. Now began one of the biggest migrations in human history, of Muslims to Pakistan and of Hindus and Sikhs to India.

Kashmir state's ruler Maharaja Hari Singh dreamed of an independent Kashmir with friendly relations with both India and Pakistan. This was not acceptable to Pakistan, which believed that due to the Muslim majority of Kashmir Valley, Kashmir should merge with Pakistan.

Within days of the Partition of India, Pakistan hatched a plan to annex Kashmir by force. It enticed tribal lashkars to attack Kashmir and fight along with the regulars of Pakistani Army led by Pakistani army officers. The lashkars were promised as much wealth and as many women they could loot, abduct and carry. They had 300 civilian lorries and enough petrol to carry back their loot and women. Pakistan had supplied them arms, ammunition and medical supplies with the connivance of the British Officers of Pakistan Army. On 20 October 1947 these lashkars attacked Kashmir from many directions. First to come under fire was Muzaffarabad and after looting and burning Muzaffarabad the invaders took over Domel and Uri.

The Maharaja sent his forces to Rajouri to defend it. Colonel Rahamatulla Khan was posted at Jhangar in command of 9 JAK Company under commander Brigadier Chattar Singh. Col. Rahamatulla Khan was ordered to recapture Sensa. 3 JAK under Maj. Nasrullah was sent to help 9 JAK. But both Col. Rahmatullah and Maj. Nasrullah deserted the Indian Army and killed their own Gurkha sepoys. Then they marched to Troachi fort held by Gurkhas under Captain Raghubir Singh Thapa and killed them too.

## 27 October: Maharaja Signs the Instrument of Accession

The situation in Kashmir deteriorated rapidly. The raiders were marching towards Srinagar. Due to the inexorable advance of the *kabailis* and Pakistani marauders, the Maharaja's dream of an independent Kashmir lay shattered. The Pakistani Army and tribal lashkars, the *kabailis* marched towards the Srinagar Airport, which was rather an airstrip, used for the landing of the Maharaja's private airplane. It was India's only air-link with Kashmir. The perfidy of Pakistan, which violated a stand still agreement with the Maharaja, and the advance of the *kabailis*, and the rebellion by his own troops and the defeat and dissolution of his forces forced the Maharaja to accede to India. On 27 October the Maharaja Signed the Instrument of Accession and asked for Indian troops. The same day Indian Armed Forces started to fly to Srinagar to defend Kashmir to save it from the clutches of the bestial laskars.

But this vacillation by the Maharaja had caused utmost suffering to his Hindu subjects of border towns of Mirpur, Bhimber, Rajouri, Kotli and Mendhar, to name a few, who bore the fury of the raiders and their own Muslim neighbours, who declared independence and set up governments of their own in the name of Azad Kashmir. These were fully supported by the attacking *kabailis* and Pakistani Army in their nefarious designs and heinous acts.

### The Sad Tale of Rajouri

Through this sad tale I want to make real the scenario in one representative town of Kashmir Rajouri. Hostilities between Hindus and Muslim's broke even before 15 August 1947, the day set for Independence of India. The worried residents of Rajouri went to the new Prime Minister Meher Chand Mahajan of J&K and requested him to send some troops to the rescue of Rajouri. He did send some units but Sheikh Abdullah, who was released from jail on Nehru's intervention, asked the troops to be sent to Reasi, where minority Muslims were being killed. There was a lava of hatred scorching lives in Kashmir. Therefore, the residents of Rajouri received no succour.

### 8th, 9th & 10 November

Where was the Indian Army? When will it come? The beleaguered people of Poonch, Naushera and Rajouri and other border town were desperately hoping that the Indian Army will come to their rescue. Everyday rumours would do rounds that the Indian Army is coming. Fearful hearts desperately prayed and hoped for the Indian Army's arrival. But alas in vain!

One day after the Instrument of Accession was signed Col. Rahmatullah and Maj. Nasrullah collected many deserters and on 28 October reached the jungles of Chacchera, near Rajouri. They knew very well the flimsy nature of the defence of Rajouri. Subedar Major

Bhim Singh was defending the town with one Gurkha Platoon and a Dogra Platoon.

On 8 November, anticipating an attack by the rebels, the Hindus of Rajouri tried to negotiate with the rebels. On behalf of the Hindu community a local leader Narsingh Dass pledged a sum of Rs. 3 crores in cash and also assured the rebel leaders that the Hindus would convert to Islam and proclaim allegiance to Pakistan. In case these proposals were not acceptable, the Hindus be allowed to take a little money for sustenance and permitted to go to Delhi. Col. Rahmatullah and Sakhi Diler turned down the offer of Hindus of becoming Pakistani citizens saying they had no authority (ikhtiar nahin hai) to accept the offer and to the offer of converting they replied that converts could never be trusted (eitbar nahin hai).

Sardar Ibrahim Khan, who had declared the formation of Azad Kashmir Government on 24 October, dispatched another contingent of rebels under the command of Sakhi Diler in the first week of November to capture Rajouri. Sadly, the Muslim citizens of Rajouri were already in touch with the invaders. On 9 November Colonel Rahmatullah Khan laid a siege around Rajouri. The local police station had only five chests of ammunition to guard the treasury and whole of the Tehsil. The brave Gurkha Platoon resisted the invaders but they became helpless as by 10 November their ammunition was exhausted. The dreaded attack came at night and the remaining Gurkha and Dogra soldiers were wiped out. The Hindus began to congregate at the Tehsil Maidan. Some prominent Muslims of the town tried to reason with Rahmatullah and Sakhi Diler to spare their Hindu neighbours, who had sought their protection. But their pleas went unheard.

A messenger was sent to the Hindus on 8 November saying that they were fully surrounded by ten thousand rebels and if they wanted a safe passage they should collect in the maidan of Baidaka with their families from where they would be allowed to go to Delhi.

The minority Hindus of Rajouri waited for the Army to come to their rescue. But the military did not reach Rajouri and the Hindus of the town realised that there end was near. Rajouri was surrounded by Azad Kashmir forces, the mujahideen, the Muslim deserters from Maharaja's Army, the Pashtoon *kabailis* and the Pakistani soldiers and officers dressed in plainclothes, the local zealots and fanatics' serfs who resented the dominant financial prosperity of the Hindus. The members of Pakistan backed Muslim Conference also supported the bestial raiders.

The Hindus had assembled in a maidan. Sensing the utter hopelessness of their situation a prominent Hindu of Rajouri Dina Nath had procured potassium cyanide from the lab of the local school as an emergency measure.

That emergency was upon them. It had been decided that if the fall became imminent, a bugle would be sounded. At the sound of the bugle first the prominent citizens and leaders consumed poison. Many men and women fell dead. But there was not enough poison to go around. Holding their infants in their arms women began jumping in the nearby river. Men began to behead their women. Some did not have any weapons. Their mothers, sisters and wives requested them to crush their heads with boulders. Instead of being violated or killed by the raiders, they preferred death at the hands of their own men. An eye witness Pishorilal writes in how women squabbled over the poison. When the poison ran out men took out axes and swords. But the swords were rusted and the men who had had never killed something bigger than a mouse, how could they kill their loved ones! Women screamed when the blows of blunt swords left them still alive. Those who did not have weapons crushed the lives of their dear ones with boulders. Many women ran to fields but were hunted and killed. It is said that 30000 to 40000 people had collected there. (*Jammu Kashmir State Ke Rajouri Nagar Ka Khooni Itihas*, by Pishorilal Jhinjotia as quoted in the book *Rajouri Remembered*, by Amar Nath Saraf p. 59.)

The raiders were circling the maidan like vultures. The homes of Hindus were burnt and many men, women and children were trapped in their homes and were burnt. Many women and children were abducted. The raiders rounded up the Hindus from the quasbas around and killed them. The raiders were ordered not to expand ammunition. Therefore, they were brutally massacred by swords, daggers and axes.

How many died that day? According to Amar Nath Saraf, "So even though the local Hindu population was around 38 thousand, at the time of the attack the numbers had risen considerably. . . Rajouri fell after three days of rioting and on 13 November 1947, the forces of occupation moved in calling themselves the War Council of Rajouri. Backed by Pakistan it set up its government. 1% of Hindus had survived." (*Ibid.*, pp. 46-47.)

The gruesome massacre began on 10 November and continued for three days. There were heaps of unclaimed bodies. After Indian Army recaptured Rajouri and later an airport was made by the Indian Air Force at the same location, during excavations thousands of skulls were found.*

On 13 November Rahmatulla nominated Mirza Mohammad Hussain to run the administration of Rajouri. A War Council was set up. This War council began to train young men to be sent for resisting the Indian forces. (*Ibid.*, pp. 44-50-53.)

**Rajouri Calling: Operation Rescue**

On 13 November 1947, the same day, when the rebels set up a War Council India launched Operation Rescue from Jammu, under the command of Brigadier Puran Jappi who arrived at Kotli on 15 November and captured Jhanger on 26 November. As it was not possible to hold the area from Beri Pattan to Kotli with one brigade his forces evacuated the refugees immediately. (*Ibid.*, p. 55.)

To recapture the sacred land of Kashmir, Indian soldiers would lay down their lives again and again. This pure oblation would be accepted by Durga and Kashmir would be rid of the raiders.

---

* Later Bakshi Gulam Mohammad gave a portion of land in the Ahta Tehsil of Rajouri to construct a memorial to the women who had sacrificed their lives in this collective jauhar. A memorial stands there now and a commemorative meeting is held on the date of the fall of Rajouri. (*Ibid*, p. 78.)

"On 16 November orders were issued to launch a two pronged simultaneous attack from Uri and Jammu for the relief of Poonch by 161 Infantry Brigade and the relief of Naushera, Jhangar, Kotli, and Mirpur by 50 Para Brigade respectively. . . . 50 Para Brigade under Brigadier Paranjape advancing from Jammu captured Jhangar on 19 November without opposition. Advance to Kotli thereafter made slow progress due to numerous roadblocks." (*A Nation Divided and the 1947 Indo-Pak War,* by Major General (Retd.) L. S. Lehl, PVSM, VrC, in the book *The Indian Army, A Brief History*, p. 69.)

Fighting murderous odds, the Indian Army inched forward. Column after column were ambushed, attacked and bridges were set on fire. The raiders attacked a relief column of Indian Army with about 200 vehicles. It was truly an uphill task for Indian Armed Forces. Poonch was under siege for one year. There were 2000 State Force personnel, 1(Para) Kumaon and 40,000 refugees in Poonch. The garrison depended on air support. "Brigadier Pritam Singh constructed an airstrip with the help of refugees for landing Dakotas to permit air supply. The legendary Air Commodore (Baba) Meher Singh, DSO, made the first landing at this short improvised airstrip carrying essential supplies in full view of the enemy from the surrounding hills. . . . Dakotas with improvised bomb fittings kept the heads of the enemy down in the neighbouring hills by bombing them. The enemy made three desperate attacks to capture Poonch but Pritam frustrated each with major losses to the enemy." (*Ibid.*, p. 70.)

## Brigadier Mohammad Usman: A Bright Son of India

Brigadier Usman was born in Uttar Pradesh. After the Country's partition, as he was a Muslim, the Pakistani Army pressured him to join them, but he remained faithful to Mother India, the land of his birth. He was to play a major role in the 1947-1948 war of Kashmir and a special role in the capture and re-capture of Jhanger. Brigadier Usman will be remembered as one of the bravest soldiers of 1947-48 War. His joy and élan of battle were contagious. He inspired his soldiers to give their best, to give their lives. He would be later awarded a Maha Vir Chakra posthumously.

On 5 November, Maj. Gen. Kalwant Singh became GOC Jammu and Kashmir Force and took charge of all Indian troops in Jammu & Kashmir. Under Brigadier Usman one brigade of our Army reached Naushera. Brigadier Usman had established pickets on important features and strengthened the defences of Naushera with mines and barbed wire. He dominated no-man's-land by his aggressive patrolling. When death dances before their eyes, the valiant welcome it with open breast. For soldiers to embrace death is the ultimate oblation in their love for the country. Usman being a soldier par excellence had inspired all the soldiers of his garrison to prepare themselves for victory or death in the coming battle and to fight like worthy sons of Mother India.

During December, the enemy kept up the pressure against our garrisons at Uri, Poonch and Jhangar. On 24/25 December night the enemy attacked Jhangar in massive numbers. They were supported by mortar and heavy automatic weapons. They captured Jhangar on 27 December 1947 and forced Brigadier Usman's forces to retreat. After the fall of Jhangar the enemy was tightening its hold around Naushera. An attack seemed imminent. Even though our troops were expecting an attack, when it happened it was much more ferocious than they had anticipated. The enemy had silently crawled around to encircle our defences. They launched a synchronised attack on all the defended localities. There was intense and continuous shelling. Our Army fought valiantly but the invaders captured Matlassi, the feature that dominated Jhangar Road. Our Army retreated in small groups to Naushera. We lost armoured cars, heavy weapons and vehicles. The platoon of 1 Mahar fought to the last man and last round but before their martyrdom they extracted a heavy price from the enemy. The enemy left behind 1000 dead. (*Ibid.*, pp. 71-72.)

Naushera Township lies at the junction of Jammu-Jhangar road and Rajuori-Naushera road. On north, south and east it is surrounded by high mountains. Brigadier Usman established pickets on important points. He also ordered mines and barbed wire planted around Naushera and aggressive patrolling of no-man's land. On 6 February the enemy attacked on all the defended localities. A section of our Howitzers had moved out on a road clearing mission. Usman ordered Col. HS Virk DSO to return to "Brigade defensive box" with the Howitzers.

Brigadier Usman's troops were under intense pressure. Apart from the numerical advantage of the enemy, soon our troops' ammunition was exhausted. There were frantic SOS calls from the units. In a brilliant move Brigadier Usman ordered the company of 3 Rajputs to reinforce the platoon on Tain Dhar or to capture it. There was intense fighting at Tain Dhar. Here Naik Yadunath Singh in spite of being wounded, repulsed the attackers from his section and won a posthumous Param Vir Chakra. Meanwhile 3 Rajput Company under their valiant leader Major Gurdial Singh hurried up to face the invaders. Upon seeing these fresh troops the enemy at Tain Dhar ran away in panic, leaving their dead and wounded behind. Now Usman ordered Col. Virk to launch an attack on the enemy in Radian area. When the tribals saw the Marathas advancing with their bayonets fixed, they ran away.

It was a great victory. Gen. Lehel writes, "The Battle of Naushera, with nearly 2,000 enemy dead and wounded, was a personal victory for Usman." (*Ibid.*, p.72.)

The next step was to recapture Jhanger. In the first week of March Major General Kalwant moved to Naushera and fixed 15 March for the advance to Jhanger. On March 15 when two companies descended in a narrow valley to evaluate the situation, from behind a ridge the enemy commenced heavy fire. Alas, both the company commanders were killed. Usman ordered to bring back the companies. Captain SC Sinha (Later Major General) extricated the companies including the dead and wounded under cover of artillery and MMG covering fire.

Lt. Col. HS Virk got Brigadier Usman's permission not to yield any ground gained by his troops. The next attack was fixed for 17 March. After a constant advance our troops took control of Matlassi Hill overlooking Jhanger. On a cold windy moonlit night Brigadier Usman reached the top of Matlassi. Marching day and night his troops secured the Matlassi High Ground over-looking Jhangar at 4 p.m. The 19 Infantry Brigade secured Jhangar on 18 March.

### Jhangar Recaptured: Brigadier Usman Sleeps on a Charpoy: Free Rum

When Jhanger had been taken by the enemy Brigadier Usman had vowed that he will not sleep on a charpoy before recapturing Jhanger. He had promised his troops free rum, if they recaptured Jhanger. Now having recaptured Jhanger the officers felt that their Brigadier should no more sleep on the ground and deserved to sleep on a charpoy. They located an old charpoy and covered it with some mule blankets, a sheet and a pillow. Then they lifted their beloved Brigadier and carried him to the charpoy.

The soldiers complained that the free rum that the Brigadier had promised his troops as a reward on recapturing Jhanger was no-where in sight. The supply column had not yet reached the Matlassi top. The irrepressible Brigadier Usman himself chased up the mules carrying supplies. And within two hours the soldiers were given their promised reward. After the rum and some *sakarparas* the troops broke out in a spontaneous Bhangra dance led by Major (later Brigadier) Sucha Singh MC. (*Ibid.*, p. 73.)

Little did the triumphant troops realise that their beloved hero of Jhangar, Brigadier Usman was to die by an enemy shell on 3 July 1948, at the foot of Matlassi. India salutes the flamboyant and indomitable Brigadier Usman.

## The Turning Point: Liberation of Rajouri

The victory at Jhanger electrified our troops in the Jammu Sector. The commanders and troops were in an upbeat mood. Their next urgent task was the liberation of Rajouri situated 50 km from Naushera. The offensive to capture Rajouri was planned by General Kalwant Singh and involved General Kariappa.

### The Road Blocks on the Way to winning a Param Vir Chakra

In this mission of liberating Rajouri, the hero of this tale Sec. Lt. Rama Raghoba Rane was to play an important part and write a glorious chapter of tenacity, sustained courage and indomitable will under the most trying conditions. Sec. Lt. Rama Raghoba Rane's was not a great act done in a moment of élan; it was an act of utmost courage and tenacity shown over a protracted period of three days, which would leave a deep footprint on the course of events, leading to the victory of India and its just cause. But more of it a little later.

### To Recapture Rajouri 8 April 1948

After recapturing Naushera and Jhangar from the *kabaili* raiders and repulsing successfully the formidable Pakistani counter attack, the Indian Army decided to take the offensive. Our troops had to capture Barwali Ridge, Chingas and finally Rajouri. Brigediar Yadunath Singh was entrusted with this mission. He was put in command of a squadron of Central India Horse. On 8 April 1948 an Indian column under Brigadier Yadunath Singh began its advance from Naushera through Barwali Ridge, towards the beleaguered town of Rajouri, where the Hindu residents had been exterminated through death, rape, loot and arson. Brigadier Yadunath Singh's task was extremely hazardous because the armed tribesman (*kabailis*) had heavily mined the road and put up huge road-blocks.

### Clearing the Land Mines: a Superhuman Task: An Indomitable Courage

This dangerous task of clearing the Mines, the demolished culverts and huge road blocks was entrusted to a section of the 37 Assault Field Company under the command of Second Lieutenant Rama Raghoba Rane. This section marched ahead of the column. It cleared the road of mines and blocks for the Indian troops and reached Nadpur, which is a strategically important place on Naushera-Rajouri Road. An enemy picket had entrenched itself in the nearby Barwali ridge and was guarding the road.

When Sec. Lt. Rane's section began to clear the road the enemy opened 3 inch mortar fire. Despite the heavy shelling Lt. Rane and his men continued their work and cleared the road of mines and blocks. Four men of his party were killed and the rest were injured.

But by the Grace of God Rane remained unscratched. He stopped the column and asked for relief.

But there was no question of stopping. The position in Rajouri was desperate. Each moment counted. Delay would result in the death of the handful of Hindus that were still alive. To advance further it was necessary to capture the picket raining shells from behind the Barwali ridge. But unluckily the picket was protected by hundreds of mines and boulders on the slopes of the surrounding area. To top it all the enemy was entrenched on commanding heights. Without waiting for relief to arrive Lt. Rane went forward defusing mines and removing blocks, ignoring the hazard to which he was exposed. At last the road was cleared and Indian column also captured the enemy picket on the Borwali Ridge. Thus the Indian Army marched for eight miles.

**Three Days under a Tank: A big Road Block**

Now our column faced another road block. From their perches in the adjoining hills the enemy guarded all the approaches to this road. The troops could not march forward till it was blasted. To make the task almost impossible there were enemy pickets posted on the adjoining hills and were guarding all the approaches to the block. The block was located in a position where it could not be bypassed.

Lt. Rane took an unheard of step that needed supreme, dauntless courage. He had himself tied to the underbelly of the leading tank. Two ropes were tied to his wrists which were held by someone sitting in the tank. If he detected a mine, he gestured with a hand to stop the tank and then defused the mine. When the road was clear he would signal with the other hand to advance. (Those who have seen the Chetan Anand serial on Param Vir Chakra Recipients can never forget the sight of the actor under the belly of the tank.)

Crawling like reptiles, Lt. Rane and his helpers cleared mine after mine, while under intense shelling by the enemy. A tank with Rane sheltered under it, inched up to the road block and Rane laid explosives and blasted it. As he crawled bullets whizzed past and shells exploded around, and killed others of Bombay Engineers who were defusing the deadly mines. Their bodies torn into countless pieces by the deadly shells, rained around Rane, his face was splattered by the sacred blood of his comrades, their heart-rending death cries rang into his ears. The echo of the sound of the bursting shells went round and round in the hills. It was a veritable dance of Kali. But Rane steeled his nerves and did not allow himself the relief of grief. His total concentration was on the deadly task ahead, of defusing the next land mine, of dismantling the next road block.

Rane crawled over a bolder-strewn path, he crawled over tangled tree branches, over shards of shells and pieces of barbed wire and broken mortar shell casings, over smouldering trees of road blocks, set on fire by exploding shells, empty casings of bullets, over mud and slush and snow, all blackened by cordite. He crawled over dead bodies of friends and enemies. With a superhuman concentration he inched forward and probed for hidden land mines. How many did he defuse? He had no time to keep a count. There were plenty of them. If even one of them had exploded he, along with the tank, would have been blown to smithereens. He removed many road blocks made out of cut trees, big boulders, debris of blown culverts and tangled barbed wire.

Rane did not eat or rest or sleep for 96 hours. As if the Goddess of War spread out her hands of protection upon this super hero to ward off the bullets and shells, those deadly harbingers of death. It seemed that nothing could touch him, and nothing did. This victorious son of Mother India was surely protected by Divine Powers to have come out alive and unscratched while four or five of his comrades in arms, doing the same work, were martyred.

Lt. Rane did this work for 96 hours, which seemed an eternity, without food or sleep. Surely some special Divine Power was protecting this incredibly brave man. The road to Chingis lay open for advancing tanks of Indian Army. Chingis was captured on 10 April 1948 and Rajouri was captured on 12 April.

Upon learning of the relentless advance of Indian Forces Mirza Mohammad Hussain of the Azad Kashmir forces retreated with thousands of raiders towards Juna. When Brigadier Yadu Nath Singh entered Rajouri, the joy of victory was clouded over by the discovery of three large pits full of the bodies of the people whom the enemy had massacred before vacating Rajouri.

(*Lt. Rane's family told Shri Rakesh Oza that from under the tank Lt. Rane also downed some Pakistani aircraft/aircrafts by mortar fire. But this fact has not been mentioned in the write-up by the Bombay Engineers.*)

## Winning of Param Vir Chakra

For his unique gallantry in the Jammu and Kashmir battle he was decorated with India's highest gallantry award The Param Vir Chakra.

## Citation

### Second Lieutenant Rama Raghoba Rane

### Bombay Engineers (SS-14246)

On 8 April 1948, Second Lieutenant Rama Raghoba Rane, Bombay Engineers, was ordered to be in charge of the mine and roadblock clearing party at Mile 26 on the Naushera-Rajouri road which passes through very hilly country.

At 1100 hours, on that date near Nadpur South, just as Second Lieutenant Rane and his party were waiting near the tanks to start the work of clearing the mines ahead, the enemy started heavy mortaring of the area, with the result that two men of the mine-clearing party were killed and five others including Second Lieutenant Rane were wounded. The officer at once reorganised his party and started work for the tanks to go on to their position. Throughout the day he was near the tanks under heavy enemy machine-gun and mortar fire.

After the capture of Barwali ridge at about 1630 hours, although knowing that the enemy had not been completely cleared of the area, Second Lieutenant Rane took his party ahead and started making a diversion for the tanks to proceed. He worked on till 2200 hours that night in full view of the enemy and under heavy machine-gun fire.

On 9 April he again started work at 0600 hours and worked on till 1500 hours when the diversion was ready for the tanks to proceed. As the armoured column advanced, he got into the leading carrier and proceeded ahead. After proceeding about half a mile he came across a road-block made of pine trees. He at once dismounted and blasted the trees away. The advance continued. Another 300 yards and the same story was repeated. By this time it was getting on to 1700 hours. The road was curving round the hill like a snake. The next roadblock was a demolished culvert. Second Lieutenant Rane again got on with the job. Before he could start work, the enemy opened up with their machine-guns, but with super courage and leadership he made a diversion and the column proceeded ahead. The roadblocks were becoming numerous, but he blasted his way through. It was now1815 hours, and light was fading fast. The carrier came across a formidable roadblock of five big pine trees surrounded by mines and covered by machine-gun fire. He started removing the mines and was determined to clear the roadblock but the armoured column commander appreciating the situation got the column into a harbour area.

On 10 April 1948 at 0445 hours, Second Lieutenant Rane again started work on the roadblock in spite of machine-gun fire with the support of one troop of tanks. With sheer will power he cleared this roadblock by 0630 hours. The next thousand yards was a mass of roadblocks and blasted embankments. .......The enemy had the whole area covered with machine-gun fire ...... with superhuman efforts, in spite of having been wounded, with cool courage and exemplary leadership and complete disregard for personal life, he cleared the road by 1030 hours.

The armoured column proceeded ahead and got off the road into the river bed of the Tawi but Second Lieutenant Rane continued clearing the road for the administrative column. The tanks reached Chingas by 1400 hours. Second Lieutenant Rane appreciating that the opening of the road was most vital, continued working without rest or food till 2100 hours that night.

On 11 April 1948, he again started work at 0600 hours and opened the road to Chingas by 1100 hours. He worked on that night till 2200 hours clearing the road ahead.

Gazette of India Notification

No. 5 – Press/50

*Being Awarded PVC by the President*

**The Hero Jumped into a well**

Apart from his extraordinary bravery mentioned above, during the 1947-48 War with Pakistan, once PVC Lt. Rane jumped into a well and saved the life of a girl.

**Great Hunter**

Rama Raghoba was a great hunter not only of enemy soldiers but also of lions. He killed seven leopards in Karvar.

## "To Marry You I Came Back."

PVC Rama Raghoba Rane was married on 3 February 1955. He told his wife Rajeshwari, "I came back alive to marry you."

## 1962: The War with China: Mangalsutra Lost

In 1962 China War while ferrying goods for the jawans, the jeep in which our hero PVC Rama Raghoba Rane was travelling, fell 5/6 thousand feet down into a ravine. While the jeep was hurtling down, with great presence of mind Param Vir Rane caught the branch of a tree and hung there. Below him was a canyon thousands of feet deep. He hung for a time that seemed an eternity, till a relief party rescued him.

At the time he fell out of the jeep at home his wife Rajeswari's mangalsutra was lost.

## Places of Posting

Param Vir Lt. Rane served in 37 Field Company till 14 August 1950. He was posted to the Centre on 15 Aug. 50 and served as Chief Transport Officer (Mechanical) till 1 April 54. He was then posted to an Infantry Division Engineers and served there as Field Force Engineering (Capt) till April 56. He again showed his mettle when he was awarded the COAS Commendation Card for devotion to duty and gallant services in Maha Prabhu Mela in Kashmir in July 54. He was then posted to a Bomb Disposal platoon as Officer Commanding till 1 July 1957. After this he was posted to another Bomb Disposal Platoon where he remained up to 3 October 57. He then went as Officer Commanding 2 National Cadet Corps Battalion (Engrs) and served in the Unit till 23 Feb 60. He worked as the Administrative Officer of Docks Operation Company (Territorial Army) and HQ Docks and Inland Water Transport (Territorial Army) till 17 Jan 68. He continued to serve the Army and on 4 Feb 69 was reemployed as Officer Commanding I Maharastra Engineer Company National Cadet Corps

*Memorial at BEG, Kirkee*

## Retirement

PVC Rane retired from NCC on 7 April 71. After an illustrious career in the Bombay Engineer Group, Maj. RR Rane, PVC (Retd.) led a retired life in Pune. Where he visited the Bombay Engineer Centre regularly.

## Family

The couple had four children, three sons and one daughter. Their eldest son Ajit is a colonel in the Army. Second son Prahalad is a mechanical engineer, the third son Rajendra is also an engineer based in Pune. Their daughter Ujjvala Sandeshmahatye did LLM from Cambridge University and is now New Jersey based.

## Unusual Similarities with Victoria Cross Winner Premindra Singh Bhagat

Maj. Gen. Ian Cardozo, in his book, *Param Vir Our Heroes in Battle* has pointed out a strange case of similarities between Premindra

Singh Bhagat, who won a Victoria Cross during Second World War in 1941 and Maj. Rama Raghoba Rane, who won the Param Vir Chakra during 1947-48 Indo-Pak War.

Gen. Cardozo points out the following similarities:

1. Both were Second Lieutenants when they won their respective awards.
2. Both were officers of Bombay Engineers.
3. There were several casualties in the teams of both.
4. Both won their awards for courage when clearing mines and roadblocks for a long time under heavy enemy fire to allow armoured and administrative columns to move forward.
5. Both cleared mines and demolished roadblocks for 96 hours.
6. By the Grace of God both survived.

Gen. Cardozo writes, "Is the similarity of their respective acts of gallantry in different wars on different continents, and at different times a coincidence or is it that one was so inspired by the other that he walked in his footsteps with his own lamp of courage lighting the way for the continuance of a tradition set by his illustrious predecessor?" (*Param Vir, Our Heroes in Battle*, Maj. Gen. Ian Cardozo, pp. 59-60.)

**A legend passes away**

Maj. RR Rane, PVC (Retd.), the only Param Vir Chakra winner of the Corps of Engineers of the Indian Army peacefully died at 2. AM on 11 July 1994 at Command Hospital Pune after a brief illness. His last rites were done with full military honours.

*Bombay Sappers get Rane's PVC from his wife Rajeshwari Rane (84), the wife of late Major Rama Raghoba Rane, handed over his Param Vir Chakra, to the Army Chief General MM Naravane.*

## Pledge of an Indian Soldier

O Beloved Country,
O Goddess beautiful
Mother India!
I belong to Thee and Thee alone
To uphold Thy honour,
To the last breath, I will fight.
At Thy altar, with joy
I offer my heart, my life,
For Thee I live and if need be,
Willingly will die,
So that Thy children –
Boys, girls, young and old –,
Undisturbed may sleep,

So that inviolate remain
Our boundaries,
Our sacred land.
Our Mother Beautiful!

Thy high mountains taught me
To hold my head high
With lofty ideals to touch the sky,
For Thee, I will pay any price.
One day, I hope, Thy children
Will be great and wise,

And each to the summit will rise.
Thy heroes Rama and Krishna
Inspired me to fight

For our just cause and hold high
Our sacred flag, our dear Tricolour.
Never will I leave Thee
To serve some other land,
Never will I go
To serve another master
Or owe allegiance to others.

I belong to Thee and Thee alone.
For Thee, I live and strive.
Though bullets pierce my body
And shells shred my flesh,
My post never will I leave,

In India's high destiny, I believe.
With my bare hands
Ten enemies will I kill,

Extract the full price
From those who violate
Our sacred country.

Soldiers are we
Of the proud Indian Army,
We stand as sentinels
On the mountain peaks,
Wade through snow and sleet
In the savage cold.
March through dry deserts
Swim through raging torrents.
Even if maimed or killed,
We are the proud soldiers
Of the Indian Army,
Born to sacrifice our all
For the great and beautiful
Goddess, Mother India.

# Major Shaitan Singh

## Birth and Childhood

In Rajasthan, on the auspicious date 1 December 1924 a child was born to Smt. Jawar Kunwar and Lt. Colonel Hem Singh in Banasar village of Falodi Tehsil of Jodhpur district. The fond parents had no inkling that their son will one day win India's highest award of bravery and this auspicious village will be one day called after their son 'Shaitan Singh Nagar'.

Yes, they gave rather an unusual name "Shaitan Singh" to their son. Roughly translated that means "Naughty Lion". It was a strange name and later in life caused much inconvenience to the child. Some people made fun of the name and some refused to believe that it was his real name. They thought that the boy was making a fool of them. Of this more later on.

Lt. Col. Hem Singh, an officer in the Army of the state of Jodhpur, had fought valiantly in the First World War and was wounded in

France. There he was instrumental in turning the tide of a battle. For his exceptional bravery, the grateful British Government conferred several honours upon him, including an OBE (Order of British Empire). In 1947 after India gained its independence, the Jodhpur State Army was merged in the Indian Army where Hem Singh OBE served with distinction and before retirement he rose to be a Lt. Colonel.

Naturally, young Shaitan Singh was greatly influenced by his father. He admired his father's qualities of leadership, bravery, dedication and honesty. Many a time he heard from his father the stories of the great battles of the First World War in which he had participated. Thus bravery was in Shaitan Singh's blood and fame was his inheritance.

## Education

Shaitan Singh studied up to matriculation in the Rajput High School, Chaupasani, at Jodhpur. Today, his full size photograph graces the big hall of the Rajput High School. At that time an Englishman A.P. Cox was its principal. This residential school was famous for its discipline and excellence in sports. Govind Singh, an old student of this school had won a Victoria Cross in the First World War. Many of the students of this school joined the Indian Armed Forces.

In an article, Shri Narayan Singh Bhati, a class fellow of Shaitan Singh wrote about him, "Many years we lived together in Pratap (boarding) House. I had the good fortune of coming in close contact with him. He spoke little and led a very simple life. Anger was foreign to his nature, yet he was fearless. His life was truly guileless and pure. He was so simple that people hesitated to cut jokes with him.

"In 1943 after passing high school he enrolled in Jaswant College. There was no change in his character and life in college. He lived a pure life and was respected by other students. In 1942 he was a member of the team in All India Labhshankar Football Challenge, which stood second. . . ." (*Rastravir Major Shaitan Singh*, pp. 4-5.)

## What a Name!

The name Shaitan Singh means 'naughty lion'. The first half of this name was the very opposite of his character. He was much too simple, quiet and gentle to do mischief. But the second half of his name 'Singh' which means 'lion', describes him perfectly. In battle he will prove himself a lion. One of his teachers had seen the spark inside the simplicity of this quiet boy. He used to say, 'One day Shaitan will do some great "mischief." 'These words will be proven true on 18 November 1962.

Yet, many a time, the name landed our hero into piquant situations. His class fellow and later colleague in Army Col. Mansingh remembers, "Once in 1954 myself and Major Shaitan Singh had come to Jodhpur on leave. One evening we both came out for a stroll and went to a bicycle shop. Shaitan Singh asked for a bicycle on rent and gave his name. The shopkeeper looked at him with disbelief, thinking that the young man was a prankster. He said, "Is it your true name or is it some kind of a joke?" Ultimately I gave my name instead and took the cycle. Later he even thought of changing his name.

"I reassured him and joked, 'This is a dangerous name. Once heard nobody can forget it. Maybe one day the whole of the Indian Army will know this name.'" How prophetic were the words of Col. Mansingh! (*Ibid.*, pp. 10-11.)

## Early Marriage

In those times Thakurs of Rajasthan were married early. Our hero was married after passing matriculation to Smt. Sugan Kanwar, daughter of Shri Jagmal Rathore of Village Amla. But nobody remembers the year of marriage. Later a son Narpat Singh was born to the couple.

## An Excellent Sportsman

Not only the students of Rajput High School Chaupasani, but whole of Jodhpur knew of Shaitan Singh as an exceptionally good football player. Colonel Mohan Singh, who belonged to Jodhpur royal family, was impressed by Shaitan Singh's expertise in games.

He saw the possibilities in this boy and asked him, "What do you plan to do?" Shaitan Singh answered that he wanted to be a lawyer. Colonel Mohan Singh advised him to enlist in the Army. This timely suggestion would give a Hero to Indian Army. He agreed and Colonel Mohan Singh appointed him as a cadet in the Durga Horse Unit of Jodhpur Lancers. (*Ibid.*, p. 68.)

## Military Career

In 1947, after India's Independence the different State Forces were merged in the Indian Army. On 1 August 1949 our hero was commissioned in the Kumaon Regiment of the Indian Army. His officers were impressed by his disciplined personality. His work during Naga Hills operations and Goa Action was appreciated and by 1955 he became a captain. In June 1962 he was promoted to the rank of a major.

## The Background of the 1962 Indo-China War

Sometimes a nation chooses a leader with a utopian world-view, who overlooks the harsh realities of the world as it is. In the consciousness of such a person pragmatism takes a back seat and he, in his simplicity and ignorance, reposes confidence in devious and diabolical persons or nations. India in 1947, due to the overriding love of Mahatma Gandhi for Jawahar Lal Nehru, chose him as Prime Minister over Sardar Patel. Thus the Nation chose one who could not gauge the perfidious Chinese mentality. For 15 years Nehru and his favourite Defense Minister Krishna Menon, instead of strengthening and expanding the Indian Army, downgraded, defanged and demoralised it and then ordered this toothless Army to throw out the numerically, as well as militarily superior and highly motivated Chinese Army from the Himalayas. It was a tragic scenario, a sure recipe for a Himalayan disaster!

## Sardar Patel's Letter Ignored: Blind Trust on China

Up to July 1962 the Chinese Government kept up the charade of eternal friendship with India. They coined the popular slogan

"Hindi-Chini, Bhai-Bhai", (Indians and Chinese are brothers.), but at the same time prepared for war. Sardar Vallabh Bhai Patel, with his uncanny foresight had written a letter to Nehru, highlighting the evil intentions of China and how India needed to be wary of China. But unluckily Nehru ignored that letter. Since Independence in 1947 Nehru had systematically reduced the man power of Indian Army and its capacities. (I remember how happy we ignorant followers, nay, worshippers of Gandhi's Non-Violence and Nehru's Non-Alignment, were when we read that the ordinance factory in Kanpur was making thermos flasks instead of ammunition. – The Author)

In 1947, when India gained independence, she inherited land boundaries with China which were marked on maps but not demarcated on the ground and worse still, not agreed to by China. In 1949 a communist government was formed in China. In 1950 China attacked Tibet. Now tensions between China and India surfaced. India moved up and brought Tawang firmly under its control. China on the pretext of effective control of Tibet, began to build a motorable road from Sinkiang to Tibet through the Aksai Chin. India was blissfully ignorant of this, until upon completion of the road in 1947, reports about this road appeared in the Chinese press. These reports had maps which showed not only Aksai-Chin but also the area south of Macmahon Line till the foothills of the Himalayas as Chinese territory. There was uproar in Indian Parliament. But the Chinese persisted in deceiving the Indian Government by saying; these were minor matters, which can be settled through talks.

Up to July 1962, outwardly the Chinese professed an undying friendship for India. When General Thorat prepared a plan for the defense of North East Federal Agency (NEFA), Nehru brushed it aside.

After 1961, Nehru, who had continuously neglected the Army and systematically destroyed its capacities, suddenly in the mistaken belief that China will never attack India, asked the Indian Army to establish 24 new posts on the cruel heights of Himalayas. The 33 Corps Commander Lt. Gen. Umrao Singh was not in favour of this aggressive policy. The Army Chief General Thimmaya advised against this step because he correctly argued that since there were no roads to supply food, arms or ammunition to the soldiers who would be posted there, these posts will be indefensible. But ignoring his sane counsel Nehru chose to challenge the Chinese by asking the Army to establish these posts in disputed territories. Thus was set the stage for the 1962 ignominious India-China War.

How wrong Nehru was is proved by a letter of Lord Mountbatten written to Lt. Gen. (then Major General) ML Chibber, (Retd.) PVSM, AVSM, PhD., on 27 September 1977. The following excerpts from this letter shows how Nehru ignored the sane advice of even such an acknowledged expert of warfare and politics as Mountbatten, who, though he was an instrument for the partition of India, and by no means a friend of India, had warned Nehru about his China policy and had forewarned him about the bitter realities of International politics and evil designs of China. He had advised against his policy of making the Indian Army toothless and unprepared for a war. If Nehru had accepted Mountbatten's advice the debacle of 1962 would not have happened. Even more pernicious was the downgrading of Indian Army by Nehru and Krishna Menon.

Broadlands, Ramsey, Hampshire

S.05.9.Z.D.

27 September 1977

Dear Chib,

Thank you so much for your letter of the 20 September which I have read with the greatest of interest.

The last time Nehru stayed with me here at Broadlands before the Chinese invasion on the North East Frontier, I urged him to appoint General Thimayya to be the CDS right away as I could see trouble brewing up. . . . I told him that the real danger was that Krishna (the then Defense Minister Krishna Menon) was appointing people like Thapar as CGS who was a good administrator but had no command experience and worse still, Kaul who appeared to be a political appointment, though he had been a personal friend.

I warned him that if war came the Indian Army would suffer a quick defeat. He said there was no question of there being a war as India wished to be at peace with everybody. To this I replied that it took two sides to decide whether there would be a war or not and if either China or Pakistan were to invade they would have a war on their hands.

He replied that he relied on his agreement with Chou in Lai and the Chinese would never invade. I questioned this and then I said, "If you are so certain you are going to have no war, why don't you cut down your armed forces and save money?"

This, however, he was unwilling to do as Krishna was against it.

I then said, "Well, when you do get involved in a war I will do everything I can to help you."

When the Chinese invaded the first thing I did was to send out Field Marshal Sir Richard Hull, then the CGS, in a Britannia which I had loaded to the very brim with self-loading rifles, as I knew the Indian Army had no up-to-date small arms.

The next thing I did was to send out my two Intelligence Officers who were extremely high-class and did co-ordination with other Intelligence Services, to try and re-organise the Military Intelligence branch which had faded right away under the influence of the remarkable Sikh whose name I forget, who ran the Government Intelligence Service.

I came out myself a bit later on and met the Defense Council and Senior Officers . . . (Courtesy *Viewpoint*, Vol.16, April-June 2001.)

## The Battleground:

On 20 October 1962 the Chinese attacked many of these newly established posts. On 21 October they repeatedly attacked Sirijap, a post being held by a company of 1/8 Gorkha Rifles under the command of Major Dhan Singh Thapa. The Gorkhas repulsed two attacks but finally the post fell to repeated Chinese attacks. Only seven members of the 1/8 Gorkha Rifles came out alive. Major Dhan

Singh Thapa was taken a prisoner and was later, after his release, awarded the Param Vir Chakra.

## Importance of Chusul

It was rightly assumed by those in charge of the battle that the next objective of the enemy will be Chusul. Chusul is a small Ladakhi village in a narrow 40 km long and 6-7 km wide, sandy valley at 14230 feet. It is flanked by the towering 19000 feet mountain-ridges of the Ladakh Range on the western side and the 22000 feet Pangong Range on its eastern side. In 1962 it was an important strategic target for the Chinese Army because India had made there an all weather landing airstrip. This airstrip was of crucial importance for the defense of whole of Ladakh. Also Chusul had a strategic location on the just completed road linking Chusul to Leh. It is located less than 15 km from the Chinese claim line and is situated almost midway between Leh, the capital city of Ladakh and Rudok, the key Chinese launching base, which is situated about a 100 km to the southeast of Chusul. It controlled the strategic Spanggur gap. On the north of Spanggur gap lay 4808 meters high **Gurung Hill**, on the South lay 5182 meters **Maggar Hill** and southeast from Chusul, 5005 meters or about 16300 feet high lay **Rezang La**.

## The Defense of Chusul: To the Last Man, the Last Bullet

Till September 1962, the defense of all of Ladakh was entrusted to the 114 Brigade of Indian Army, which consisted of just two infantry battalions; 1/8 Gurkha Rifles and 5 Jat. Initially, only the Gurkhas were deployed in Chushul. Now this heroic task was entrusted to a Kumaon Regiment officer Brigadier (later Army Chief) TN 'Tappy' Raina, MVC. He had orders to defend Chusul, the vital battle ground to the last man, last bullet. He flew into Chusul on 28 October 1962. His brigade was responsible for the defense of a daunting 80 km stretch of towering Himalayan mountainous region. After an inspection of the battle-zone Brigadier Raina at once realised that the Chinese could attack Chusul by occupying the eastern heights of Gurung Hill, Maggar Hill and Rezang La. He entrusted the task of defending Chusul to 13 Kumaon Regiment, with one of its companies at Rezang La. At the time 13 Kumaon was at Baramulla, in the Kashmir Valley. Its Commanding Officer, Lt Col HS Dhingra was being treated in the military hospital. But upon getting the news of the new orders, he simply walked out of the hospital as his unit was going to war. Upon reaching Chusul Lt Col HS Dhingra began the deployment of 13 Kumaon Battalion. 13 Kumaon was an old Paltan and had a glorious military record. Lt Col HS Dhingra appointed Charlie Company of the 13 Kumaon, led by Maj. Shaitan Singh, to defend the critical sector of Rezang La, which was situated 10 km from his Battalion Headquarters. It was the Kumaon Regiment's only all-Ahir battalion; its hardy men of farming stock; coming from the Gurgaon/Mewat/Mahendergarh/Rewari Ahirwal belt of Haryana.

## The Build up to the Battle of Chusul

HQ 15 Corps had approved of Gen Budh Singh, GOC of the just raised 3 Infantry Division at Leh, recommending Chusul as the **Vital Ground** foreseeing that if the Chinese intended to take Leh, then the Spanggur Gap between the mountains in which Chusul lies, would be their obvious route. 114 Infantry Brigade, till September 1962 a two battalion Brigade tasked to defend the whole of Ladakh, thus suddenly found itself tasked to defend Chusul with four battalions under Brigadier TN 'Tappy' Raina. He was ordered to defend this **Vital Ground** to the last man, last bullet. He flew into Chusul on 28 October 1962. His area of responsibility was from Lukung in the north to Tsaka La in the south; a formidable 80 km stretch in high altitudes of the Himalayas.

Brigadier Raina assessed that the Chinese had three attack options for Chusul; from the north (Lukung/Thakung area); from across the Pangong Tso; and, lastly, integrated infantry/armour attacks launched from Rudok, which provided road access up to the Spanggur Gap, along with the option of cutting off the Indian road communications near Tsaka La. This he considered most likely. He realised that defending Chusul could be done by holding the western heights of the valley (in that case the airstrip would be compromised) or occupying the eastern heights (Gurung Hill, Maggar Hill and Rezang La). He chose the latter option. His final deployment was to hold the northern approach (Lukung) with 1 J&K Militia; the southern (Tsaka La) approach with 5 JAT, Gurung Hill with 1/8 Gurkha Rifles supported by two troops of AMX-13 tanks of 20 Lancers which had been airlifted by AN-12B aircraft to Chusul on 26 October and the Maggar Hill-Rezang La complex with 13 Kumaon, with one of its companies at the site of the current Rezang La memorial in the valley.

Chusul proper was protected by the half squadron of light tanks, the recoilless guns of the Brigade; a battery of 13 Field Regiment and a troop of 32 Heavy Mortar Regiment, as also a lot of camouflaged dummies made of abandoned dozers and other unserviceable vehicles. The Brigade Head Quarter was on the high ground overlooking the airstrip, protected by the Battalion HQ of 1/8 Gurkha Rifles and a section of Mahar Regiment's Medium Machine Guns.

## When China Attacked Rezang La

Rajasthan is the land of bravery. Here were born brave hearts, a handful of whom would put on saffron robes and willingly go out on suicidal missions to fight thousands of enemy soldiers. They fought to the last breath. It is said that such was the will and momentum in their hearts that in some exceptional cases, even when the heads were severed, the hands of the dead soldiers went on wielding their swords.

Though they wore not saffron, but standard Military green uniforms, the self-sacrifice of the proud Charlie Company of the 13 Kumaon Regiment at Rezang la was no less great than that of the ancient Rajputs. Major Shaitan Singh's Charlie Company was no ordinary company. Just five months before the '62 War this company had won a defence prepared competition at Baramulla.

During war what matters greatly is the cohesion of the soldiers, the close bonding amongst them, the total concern their leader has for them and in return their respect, devotion to and love for their leader. If this is present then the whole unit is so well-knit that it becomes like a single burning torch of love for the motherland, where one cares less for one's own self than for one's buddies, for one's leader and above all for one's own country. Charlie Company was such a unit, where each soldier offered himself like a crimson flower of bravery, ready to be offered at the lotus feet of Mother India. And for this willingness for self sacrifice, this utter disregard for oneself, a major credit goes to the soft spoken, quiet warrior and ideal leader Major Shaitan Singh, who implicitly obeyed the orders of his Brigadier Raina "To the last round and the last man".

And like Maj. Shaitan Singh, when the time came, his soldiers did not flinch from death, even though the odds were piled up against them sky high. There was no idea of turning back. Death can not defeat such warriors; it glorifies them so much that on the pages of history books, their names stand out as living beacons. They are more alive than the millions who live for their own well being, never caring for the motherland. These millions, whatever their wealth or position, are valueless ciphers for the country and its high Gods.

## Four Letters of Hope and Reassurance

The hallmark of a hero is his capacity to face the worst of odds with a cheerful disposition. Here we present four letters our hero Major Shaitan Singh wrote when he knew that death was not only a possibility, not only a probability but almost a certainty. Rushed in from Baramulla to Ladakh, the 13 Kumaon had begun its deployment on 24 October 1962.

The curtain was to fall on the Charlie Company on 18 November, only 24 days away. As we have seen that the orders given to them by their battalion commander were stark, "To the last man and the last bullet." The greatest disadvantage for C Company of Major Shaitan Singh was that in case of a Chinese attack, due to the surrounding high ridges, they could not get artillery support from their battalion, while the Chinese Army had full artillery support. The men of Charlie Company were isolated and cut off from succour. These 124 brave hearts under their indomitable Major Shaitan Singh were completely on their own. Their arms and ammunition were unsuitable and insufficient. The enemy was better placed, better armed, greater in numbers, had a road network, by which they could ferry troops, arms, ammunition by trucks right up to front line. In contrast, our troopers of Charlie Company carried their limited ammunition, 40 pounder tents, rations and whatever tools could be mustered, on the back of yaks and mountain ponies hired from the local Ladhakis.

Yet Major Shaitan Singh was serene and the morale of his men was sky high. Ram Chander, one of the six survivors of Rezang La and the last man to talk with mortally wounded Major Shaitan Singh, now in his mid seventies, recounted how their immediate tasks done, the troops along with Major Shaitan Singh gathered around the radio to listen to news from All India Radio. Upon hearing how the Chinese were attacking our posts and killing our soldiers, the Ahir soldiers of Charlie company would say to Major Shaitan Singh, "Sahib, Let us get a chance to fight and we will teach the Chinese a lesson they will never forget." Major Shaitan Singh would smile back.

In that most daunting scenario, the unflappable, unperturbed hero-warrior Major Shaitan Singh wrote the following three letters to his friend Shaurya Chakra winner Colonel Mal Singh. The first of these letters he had written on 9 January 1962, before coming to Chusul, when he came to know that his friend Col. Mal Singh was wounded on 18 December 1961 in Goa Action:

To

Col. Mal Singh

9 January 1962

"My dearest brother,

Jai Shri Krishana.

It gives me a very severe shock but later on immense pleasure to learn from Lt. Malhotra that though, you were severely wounded but you stood most magnificently for which you had been recommended for an award and now that you are out of danger, I congratulate you from the core of my heart for Rajput in the battlefield.

Mal Ji I assure you, you are really lucky to get an opportunity to fight, where as I did absolutely nothing."

Major Shaitan Singh's love for battle, manifest in this letter, is the hall-mark of heroes, who want to wager their lives for the country. Soon his wish would be fulfilled.

On 2 November, sitting in his tent at Rezang La, he wrote to Col. Mal Singh,

"Brother,

I am perfectly happy and in fine health. I would not know when I shall get leave? Now that is a secondary requirement. I am more than sure to meet you sometime early next year, if not this year."

On 9 November he wrote,

"I assure you Mal Ji that I am in perfect health and also in wonderful spirits."

On 11 November, 1962 he wrote,

My dearest brother

Jai Ambe.

You wrote me this letter immediately after you recovered a little and that too with your left hand; your right hand being unable to function for the present, shows not only immense love and affection you have for me but also your greatness. I am really very, very proud of you as a friend and brother.

I believe they did not or rather could not pull out quite a few bullets from your body at Jamnagar, have they pulled out now? . . ."

We must remember that these letters were written from a height of 5,500 meters (17,000 feet) in freezing cold, facing impossible odds. Yet, when death was almost a certainty, our hero writes that he was "in wonderful spirits." On 13 November 1962 the youthful Major Shaitan Singh wrote the following letter to his brother-in-law Shri Mool Singh Ji, as if death was not peeping from behind the curtain of days, that the day of supreme self sacrifice, 18 November, was only five days away. Sitting amongst snow covered mountains, he wrote:

My Dear Mr. Mool Singh Ji Sahib,

How fortunate I am to receive your most affectionate letter only yesterday.

I may assure you that I am in best of my health and in wonderful high spirits. I am where you think me to be. I may assure you I am really proud and happy to be here. We are all happy and there is no cause for anxiety. I once again thank you very much for your most affectionate letter and I would again like to assure you that I am most happy and healthy and in wonderful high spirits.

With kindest regards

Yours sincerely

Shaitan Singh

This was the positive attitude of a true soldier awaiting martyrdom, only a few days away. Interestingly during a train journey Major Shaitan Singh had met an astrologer who, after reading his palm, had predicted that he was going to achieve glory and fame.

## Battle Preparation at Rezang La

So let us turn our attention to Rezang La, the sacred site of sacrifice of 114 brave hearts of 13 Kumaon's Charlie Company. The Chinese had built a motorable track to this pass which linked it with the Spanggur-Rudok Road. The danger was that if the Chinese captured the pass they could block the road newly constructed by India to Chusul and would thus cut off the 114 Brigade, which was responsible for the Chusul defenses, from their food and ammunition supplies from Leh. To capture the Chusul complex, the Chinese first needed to capture Gurung Hill, Maggar hill and, most importantly, Rezang La, which provided the most dangerous approach to cut off this vital Chusul-Leh road. This road was the sole Indian communication life-line to Leh. Our military authorities realised that if the Chinese intended to take Leh, then their obvious route will be the Spanggur Gap between the mountains in which Chusul lies.

## The Conditions on the Battlefield

We laymen talk of heights as figures saying that the battle was fought at 15,000 feet, 16,000 feet or 17,000 feet but generally do not realise what that means in practical terms. On 31 October 2012, while in Pondicherry, on my request, Maj.Gen. Raj Mehta made concrete, the stark reality of these formidable heights, in a way which a layman can understand. He noted down the extreme cold problems at Rezang La thus:

"At 17,000 feet high altitude due to rarified air and therefore lesser oxygen content, simple things like cooking, even going through the daily regimen, take a toll.

Some Examples:

Drinking Water: First boiling takes 30 minutes.

Tea: Making tea takes up to 30 minutes.

Rice: Cooking takes up to 1 & 1/2 hours to 2 hours.

Chapati Making: Impossible

Shaving: Impossible

Toilet: It can take 1&1/2 hours to 2 hours to perform ablutions. Constipation takes a murderous toll of soldiers. Digestion gets destroyed.

(The following heroic battle account is mostly based on Maj. Gen. Raj Mehta's article: *Thermopylae Redux In High Himalayas* and Rachana Bhist Rawat's interviews with the survivors of Charlie company and the Hindi book *Rastraveer Major Shaitan Singh Smriti Granth.* - The Author)

## The Battle Commences

13 Kumaon arrived in June 1962 in Jammu & Kashmir from Ambala. They reached Leh on 2 October. After ten days they were moved to Chusul. From there they were sent to Rezang La Pass, which is

situated 30 km south of Chusul. The Charlie Company had to climb for three hours to reach Rezang La, which was situated about 10 km from the battalion HQ. It is an irony that the soldiers of this company had never seen snow before their posting to Baramulla and now they were to fight the most important and the last battle of their lives at one of the coldest and highest battlefields of the world. In contrast the Chinese soldiers were from the mountains of Sinkiang.

Charlie Company's defence preparations had begun only in the last week of October 1962. Winter had set in and it made the task of our soldiers very difficult. There was a shortage of everything (except of courage). The shortage of snow clothing and shoes made matters worse. The jerseys, cotton trousers and light coats that were issued to them could not give sufficient protection against the freezing winds. The soldiers got splitting headaches. The nursing assistant Dharam Pal Dahiya was kept on his toes, rushing from one post to another, giving medicine to the soldiers. Digging in the hard rocky surface proved so difficult that our troops piled up stones above the ground level to prepare firing positions.

Sadly the equipment of the Indian Army was not designed for operating in sub-zero temperatures. Our men had bolt action .303 rifles equipped with five round magazines and 600 rounds per soldier, six LMGs (light machine guns), some grenades and 1000 mortar bombs in all. The company had no anti-personnel mines. The Chinese, by comparison, had 7.62mm self loading rifles; MMG's (medium machine guns) and LMG's; 120mm/81mm/60mm mortars; 132mm rockets; and 75mm/57mm recoilless guns to bust bunkers. Additionally, they had the advantage of being on higher grounds.

The eternal silence of the snows of the mighty Himalayas was disturbed by this feverish activity of Charlie Company. There were no tin sheets to make shelters. Therefore our troops pitched 40 pounder tents, which would be later shredded to bits by Chinese mortars. Major Shaitan Singh also lived in one such tent. The roaring winds as if aligned with the enemy and strained against the ropes to uproot the tents. Our troops had orders that their patrols should not to go beyond international border. They were thus restricted to patrolling up to 400 yards of their post.

## The Immortal Last Stand of Maj. Shaitan Singh and Charlie Company

The Chinese had concentrated a regiment with battalions of troops, along with heavy mortars and artillery support in that sector. Dawn broke on 18 November 1962; unusually cold, with snow falling lightly over Rezang La. This day saw a battle that was unique in many ways. Never before in the world's military history had a major battle been fought at such an altitude. The forces arrayed were also unequally matched. At about 0615 hours, all those deployed around Chusul, were attracted by the sound and sight of massive shelling on Rezang La, Gurung Hill and Spanggur gap - bringing the entire Infantry Brigade posted at Chusul to their respective battle positions.

Actually, the Battle of Rezang La commenced hours before this shelling that the rest of Brigade saw from a distance. In fact, the first Chinese attack was 'silent', with the intention to surprise the defenders of Rezang La, in which, the Chinese failed. Barring incidents of mortar firing and patrolling, the real Chinese attack in the Chusul sector commenced on 18 November, with several simultaneous attacks being launched in the east. The Chinese appeared to have used nearly two battalions against Rezang La. The 13 Kumaon's Charlie Company, due to the unavailability of resources, was without artillery support and had to depend only on light 3-inch mortars. In view of its isolated position, the Company had to be prepared to face the enemy from all directions. (A battalion has three or more companies of soldiers. Each company has two or more platoons; each platoon has usually 3 sections of 10 to 12 men.)

The commander of 114 Brigade, Brig TN Raina and the battalion's commanding officer, Lt Col HS Dhingra, had visited Charlie Company several times to assess its preparedness and it was made clear to Maj. Shaitan Singh, that the company had to hold on its own to the very end if need be. The brave hero Maj. Shaitan Singh and his soldiers cheerfully accepted the challenge and faced the likelihood of martyrdom with fortitude.

## The Deployment and the First Attack

Maj. Shaitan Singh had deployed the 7 Platoon led by Jemadar Surja to the north of the pass, 9 Platoon, led by Jemadar Ram Chandra was placed 1 km south of 7 Platoon's position along with the Company HQ and 8 Platoon was deployed a further 1.5 km south. As we have pointed out before, a major disadvantage to our troops was that the defensive positions dug out in the permafrost soil and rock by his 7, 8 and 9 Platoons could not get artillery fire support when needed as the guns of Indian Army were behind the Maggar Hill complex in the Spanggur Gap. The company of 118 men was stretched over two kilometer wide pass, with wide gaps between the platoons and without shell proof overhead cover for their bunkers.

Snowfall began on the night of 17 November. At about 2 am on 18 November, forward observation posts of Charlie Company detected Chinese troops approaching. Soon, a battalion sized force attacked Rezang La from two directions, approaching the Indian positions through nullahs that led up to hill tops. Our troops opened-up with everything they had and the Chinese became sitting ducks in the nullahs to the mortar fire and the hand grenades of the jawans of Charlie Company. After about half an hour of intense firing, the first Chinese attack disintegrated. The Chinese thereafter opened up artillery fire, which though not effective, broke telephone lines and damaged the company's radio, leaving the company totally on its own, unable to call up reinforcements.

The Chinese, who embarked on a two-pronged attack to secure Chusul, struck after overrunning all Indian posts north of it. Without any warning, 13 Kumaon's three companies – came under heavy artillery fire. Maggar Hill was manned by A and B companies, both artillery positions. As we have mentioned, Major Shaitan Singh's Charlie company at Rezang La, held a 2 km frontline with 118 men. The spot's remoteness from Gurung Hill and Maggar Hill also precluded the possibility of assistance. From the very beginning,

Singh's mission was doomed to failure. It was like the olden days when Rajput warriors volunteered for a battle wearing clothes of the saffron (Kesariya) colour, signifying that it would be a battle from which there will be no return.

### Repeated Chinese Attacks

After the first attack failed, the Chinese resorted to a simultaneous attack from the rear and the southern flank under cover of an intense artillery barrage and what then followed was intense combat at close quarters. Wave after wave of Chinese troops came in and many were cut down by the Kumaonis. As the Chinese regrouped and attacked again, they brought down concentrated medium machine gun fire on Indian positions, wiping out two platoons. The Chinese then brought up a 57 mm recoilless gun and targeted our trenches one by one.

### The Extraordinary Bravery of Gulab Singh and Ram Singh

When Jemadar Surja saw that the Chinese had brought forward a MMG, he ordered Naik Ram Singh to take LMG and move forward towards some rocks with Gulab Singh. They beat back the attack. But the Chinese MMG was raining death on our jawans. It was imperative to silence it. Surja now had only 11 men left. Gulab Singh volunteered and he and Ram Singh worked their way towards the deadly MMG. It was a desperate endeavour, bound to fail but desperate situations demand equally desperate measures. As they sprinted forward towards that MMG both the volunteers fell dead, when they were only a few feet from the MMG.

The extraordinary bravery of Gulab Singh and Ram Singh impressed even the enemy. The Chinese later covered their bodies with blankets and left a "Brave Indian Soldiers" note. It was a tribute by the enemy from the heart.

### Three Choices

By this time, Maj. Shaitan Singh had to take a decisive step. He had three choices – 1. hold on to his position and fight on, 2. break out towards the rest of the battalion though at the risk of additional casualties, 3. or to surrender and save the lives of his remaining men. He realised that if he abandoned the fight, the Chinese would get easy access to Point 18,300, making it impossible for the rest of the battalion to secure the area and thereby having an adverse impact on the brigade's defensive plan.

With his company strength down to just that of a platoon, he resolved to stay put in an effort to buy more time for the brigade. The decision, according to available information, was taken knowing that he would be able to hold on only for a limited period and would eventually be overrun.

As he picked up new positions and re-deployed the remnants of his company, Maj. Shaitan Singh and two others were hit by MMG fire. Dharam Pal was the only nursing orderly with the C Company. While tending the wounded he himself was hit and wounded. As the radio was damaged earlier, they could not ask for reinforcements and thus, were totally on their own, with no possibility of contact with the headquarters. Enemy fire swept the area, decimating Indian troops. But a handful of those who still remained continued to fire their mortars and light machine guns until they were finally overwhelmed. According to one historical excerpt, as a jawan was disabling his mortar, he was hit in the arm by Chinese soldiers about 20 yards away from his command post. He went into the command post with a rifle and shot the first Chinese to enter. This was followed by several grenades being hurled into the post. And the souls of our surviving brave hearts left their bodies for their heavenly abode, ending the last of the resistance. The battle for Rezang La had lasted about five hours.

**Mortally wounded: Crimsoning the Snow**

With an advancing Chinese MMG unit mowing down Maj. Singh's soldiers by the tens, one of his men Naik Sahi Ram, managed to drop more than a hundred Chinese soldiers who had grouped to overrun the platoon. But when Shaitan Singh embarked on a recovery operation, he was felled by a sniping MMG attack that tore a hole in his stomach. This attack on his beloved Major so incensed Company Havildar Major Harpal Singh that he grabbed a LMG and shot dead the Chinese who had fired that fatal shot at Major Shaitan Singh. He was felled by the enemy fire. But before dying he told Ram Chander, "Don't let our Maj. Sahib fall in enemy hands."

By then, Major Shaitan Singh was only half conscious. He asked Ram Chander to open his belt, as it was hurting him. Ram Chander put his hand inside the Major's shirt and found that his intestines had spilled out. Ram Chander did not open his belt because the intestines would have fallen out. He tied his muffler on the wound of Major Shaitan Singh. Ram Chander held him in his arms and rolled down the ravine. He carried Major Shaitan Singh on his back for 800 meters. Then he laid down the Major, who was in mortal agony, near a boulder. There they met another jawan, who was also wounded. These two jawans picked the Major and tried to evacuate him. To send the news to the Headquarters and to save the lives of the two jawans Major Shaitan Singh asked them to leave him and to save themselves. The soldiers answered that even if they were killed they will not leave him behind. Major Shaitan Singh was more concerned with getting the battle-information to Chusul.

As life was ebbing out he said, "This is my company, I want to die here. Leave me here, save yourself. Tell them how we fought till the last. This is an order for you. *Yeh Aapke liye adesh hai.*" A soldier has to obey his commander's order. The two soldiers were now helpless. With a heavy heart they carried their gallant commander some distance and laid him next to a boulder on the slope of the hill. Major Shaitan Singh had spoken feebly as with a faint smile he bade his faithful comrades farewell. He held on to his stomach. Blood was gushing out of his fatal wound crimsoning the snow. Ultimately his arms hung limp. The injured Major froze to death during the night.

It was 8.15 a.m. The two soldiers saw destruction and death all around. The tent of the quarter master had been set to fire by their own men because they had orders to burn everything so that it may not fall in the hands of the enemy. The tent of Major Shaitan Singh was blown to pieces. With heavy hearts the two soldiers walked six miles to the battalion HQ in Chusul.

## A Footnote: Nihal Escapes

The Chinese had taken prisoner five of our soldiers. One of them Nihal escaped and walked under that dull and grey sky, ducking behind boulders, hiding amongst the shadows and somehow reached his post. His heart broke when he saw the bodies of his friends scattered around. Most poignant was the case of Mahender from Mandola Village whose legs were crushed. Mahender, upon seeing Nihal pleaded that he take him along. But Nihal's arms were bullet-riddled and he was unable to help Mahender. He showed his limp arms to Mehender. Seeing how helpless Nihal was, Mahender said, "All right brother, you cannot save me then save yourself at least." To this day it hurts Nihal that he could not help a wounded comrade. He groped his way towards Chusul. The Chinese, aware of his escape, were firing flares in the sky to spot him but his white parka blended well in the snow and the enemy could not see him. He came down the ridge, wounded and exhausted, but due to snow every thing and every stone was covered with white snow. Nihal lost his sense of direction.

Then like an angel, Tommy a dog from a village nearby, who used to come to their camp everyday to get meat, found him. Nihal dragged himself behind the dog. He tripped and fell down several times. Then the Gods of India came to the rescue of this brave soldier. The binoculars of a soldier on duty at the HQ, focused on a moving dot. On closer inspection he found that it was a wounded soldier, with tattered, bloody uniform crawling through the snow. His limp arms were hanging by his sides. One soldier identified him and mercifully he was rescued, brought into the warm shelter, given food and tea and then sent to Jammu for treatment. He recounted how the Chinese brought 25 trucks to load the bodies of more than 500 soldiers. Thus each of the Heroes of Charlie Company on an average killed 4 or 5 Chinese.

## None Had a Bullet in the Back

It is noteworthy that no one of the Company had left his position, no one had accepted defeat. None had a bullet in the back. The last stand of 13 Kumaon succeeded in blunting the Chinese assault. Thereafter, the Chinese did not push further towards the Chusul plain, which was a critical checkpoint on a potential Chinese advance on Leh. The 114 Brigade commanded by Brigadier T.N. Raina, never faced the expected next attack. The ceasefire came on midnight of November 21/22, 1962. For the 114 Ahir soldiers killed at Rezang la, the Chinese Army lost more than 1000 troops. The battle's official history states that of the 124 men deployed at Rezang La, only 14 survived. When the list of Prisoners of War came through, there were four names from 13 Kumaon on it.

After the ceasefire Rezang La was declared a disputed area, a 'no man's land' which neither country could occupy. Thus the dead of the Charlie Company lay there at rest, shrouded and frozen in snow till three months later by chance in January 1963 a shepherd, grazing his cattle in the no man's land, discovered them.

Maj.Gen. Raj Mehta writes, "In January 1963, a shepherd chanced on Rezang La. It was as if the last moments of the battle had turned into a frozen tableau. Using International Red Cross facilitation, Brigadier Raina led a team which recorded the scene for posterity with cine/still cameras. Proud Indians learnt what had actually happened on that Sunday morning. The company commander and his jawans were found in the trenches still holding their weapons; each with multiple bullet and shrapnel/bayonet wounds. The 2-inch mortar man died with a bomb in his hands; the medical orderly with a syringe in his hands. . . .993 of the 1000 mortar bombs had been fired, with the balance seven ready to be fired. Every man died a hero."

The visit disclosed 96 bodies of Kumaoni soldiers who had perished in the action. Out of 124 men who were posted to Rezang La 113 had died fighting. The remarkable fact was that none of the soldiers had a wound in his back. None tried to retreat, none tried to save himself. The body of Major Shaitan Singh was found exactly where it had been placed by his jawans. It is said that even the battle hardened

Brigadier T.N. Raina broke down because he had given the order to Charlie Company to fight up to the last man and last bullet. On 18 January the body of Maj. Shaitan Singh was brought from there and flown to Jodhpur by a special plane. The Indian Govt. wanted to bring the body of our hero to the Circuit House so that public could pay their last respects. But the family of PVC Major Shaitan Singh did not agree to the proposal. Then Col. Mohan Lal suggested that the body be brought to his house, where general public as well as the members of the Jodhpur royal family paid their respects to Major Shaitan Singh. From there the body was taken to the Cremation Ground in a procession led by ministers, MLAs, prominent men and a large number of citizens, passing through Sojati Gate and Court road to the Kaga Cremation Ground. Maj Gen. Bhagwati Singh laid a wreath on the byre on behalf of the President of India. There the body was cremated with full military honours.

After his martyrdom his mentor Col. Mohan Singh Bhati wrote, "Till then I considered myself his CO (Commanding Officer) but now Shaitan Singh is my CO and I am his soldier." *(Rastraveer Major Shaitan Singh Smriti Granth, p. 68.)*

The rest of the martyrs of 13 Kumaon were cremated in mass funeral pyres with full military honours at the place where battalion headquarters used to be at the time of battle and where the Rezang La memorial proudly stands today. There, on a white marble are inscribed the names of the martyrs of Rezang La and the following lines quoted from the poem *Horatius,* by Thomas B. Macaulay:

How can a man die better

Than facing fearful odds,

For the ashes of his fathers,

And the temples of his gods.

## Param Vir Chakra

The Government of India decided to confer the nation's highest decoration for gallantry, the Param Vir Chakra on Major Shaitan Singh posthumously.

## The Citation

### Major Shaitan Singh

### 13 Kumaon (IC 7990)

Major Shaitan Singh was commanding a Company of an infantry battalion deployed at Rezang La in the Chusul Sector at a height of about 17,000 feet. The locality was isolated from the main defended sector and consisted of 5 defended platoon positions. On 18 November 1962, the Chinese forces subjected the company position to heavy artillery, mortar and small arms fire and attacked it in overwhelming strength in several successive waves. Against heavy odds, our troops beat back successive waves of enemy attack. During the action, Major Shaitan Singh dominated the scene of operations and moved at great personal risk from one platoon post to another, sustaining the morale of his hard-pressed platoon posts. While doing so, he was seriously wounded but continued to encourage and lead his men, who, following his brave example, fought gallantly and inflicted heavy casualties on the enemy. For every man lost to us, the enemy lost four or five. When Major Shaitan Singh fell, disabled by wounds in his arms and abdomen, his men tried to evacuate him but they came under heavy machine-gun fire. Major Shaitan Singh then ordered his men to leave him to his fate in order to save their lives.

Major Shaitan Singh's supreme courage, leadership and exemplary devotion to duty inspired his company to fight gallantly almost to the last man.

Gazette of India Notification

No. 68 – Press/62

## The Glory

Thus in the Chusul plains in Ladhak was written a glorious chapter by the India Army, which some military historians compare with the famous battle fought at Thermopylae, in 480 BC, where King Leonidas with his 300 Spartan warriors had died, defending the pass against the Persian invaders.

The Commander, Brig. R Jatar, commanding the Bravo and Delta companies of 13 Kumaon on Maggar Hill had sent a patrol of four men to find out the fate of Charlie Company. Two of the scouts died, two returned to tell the tale of how the Chinese Army was using porters, wearing blue uniforms to load their dead into trucks. Twenty-five trucks were loaded opposite "Rezang La", which puts the number of Chinese dead at least at 500. Some claim that the Chinese lost 1000 soldiers at Rezang La. In 1963, when the Red Cross teams went to recover the bodies, they saw the place littered with field dressings and blood marks indicating heavy casualties suffered by the enemy. In a rare broadcast Peking radio admitted that they had suffered their highest casualties during the 1962 war at Rezang La.

At Rezang La India lost one of it's bravest of the brave companies, the redoubtable Charlie Company. In the War Diary of 13 Kumaon Regiment are noted the poignant words for that day of martyrdom 18 November 1962:

**"We are now without Charlie Company"**

The Kumaon Battalion was later awarded the **Battle Honour 'Rezang La'** and the **Theatre Honour 'Ladakh 1962'**. The battle of Rezang La is one of the most glorious chapters in the history of the Indian Army. Sadly, the last stand of 13 Kumaon at Chusul is not widely known. The story of their valour should be made a part of our textbooks. In that unequal war of 1962 against the Chinese, when the Ahir Charlie Company from 13 Kumaon, decided that until they were alive the Chinese weren't going to have a look-in on Chushul, of the 118 defenders, only three survived, seriously wounded. Their genuine 'last man-last round' defence, succeeded in stalling the Chinese advance in this sector.

Brigadier R.V. Jatar, who commanded the D Company in 1962 War said, "It is a credit to Maj. Shaitan Singh's courage, devotion to duty and leadership that his men fought so bravely till the end despite knowing the odds were against them. They did this because he was the perfect leader, who inspired them with his own example." (*The Brave*, Rachna Bisht Rawat, p. 108.)

## At Present

Rezang la bears testimony to one of the most decisive battles fought against the Chinese during that black winter of 1962. The men have long gone, having laid down their lives facing fearsome odds, but they have left behind a legacy. Sadly, great battles in India are for history books and memorials once erected with great fanfare, are left to gather dust. At least, this is what you get to see in this Haryana town Rewari, where not many seem to know even about the existence of the memorial. Where very few seem to know what happened to its Ahir soldiers at Rezang La. To them, Rewari is home only to the National Cadet Corps. Most people here will tell you that this town has nothing to do with the Army. Not even when you remind them that every 18 November, the Rezang La Shaurya Samiti conducts a ceremony to remember its heroes.

The memorial compound, located near the dusty tributary of NH-8 that bisects Rewari, is locked. There is no sign of the chowkidar. The central structure is crowned by a finger holding the Sudarshana Chakra - the Ahirs maintain they are the descendents of Krishna. But wild grass threatens the plaque, dedicated to the memory of the men who died at Chusul.

Besides the Param Vir Chakra of Major Shaitan Singh, one Mahavir Chakra, eight Vir Chakra and four Sena Medals, one Vishist Seva Padak were awarded for gallantry. Shortly after the war C-Company, 13 Kumaon was designated by a special gazette notification as the Rezang La Company.

Today Rezang La lies on the Line of Actual Control and is recognized as no man's land. At the site where the battalion headquarters of

13 Kumaon was located during the conflict, stands a memorial dedicated to the gallant soldiers of Charlie Company of 13 Kumaon.

*Memorial at Rezang La*

## Greatest Stories of Collective Bravery

The Battle Of Rezang La is listed in the 8 stories of collective bravery of all times, published by the UNESCO which also includes The Battle of Saragarhi **21 Sikh Vs 10000 Afgans** and The Battle of Thermopyle in 480 BC with just 300 Spartans against the vast Persian Army.

### In KRC War Museum : A Tribute by Maj. Gen. Raj Mehta

It was sometime in the summer of 1986. Having just attended the Staff College course, I was pleasantly surprised when ordered to report to the Kumaon Regimental Centre (KRC), Ranikhet, for correction of the Army's Part D Promotion Examination papers. I spent a week there, in that pine scented Centre in the Kumaon hills, helping correct the papers. I also spent some time during each day of my stay, visiting the KRC War Museum; one of the finest the Army had available.

There were fascinating exhibits to see but none more moving than those of Maj. Shaitan Singh, PVC (Posthumous), that held me riveted.…His blood stained uniform shirt, his bullet pierced FSMO (back-pack) and aluminum mess tin, were indisputable proof of the manner in which this bravest-of-brave hearts met his death, and, with him, almost all of his Charlie Company. I have travelled widely but do not recall any other bravery exhibits that so compel you to salute the spirit of a man who led himself and his men into the noblest of deaths; on an icy Himalayan battlefield, equipped with little more than cold courage, sheer grit and passion for **Naam, Namak** and **Nishan**. 21 years later, I visited the war memorial at Chusul, in Ladakh; the strategic area that he had died defending. …

* * *

Tributes from highly placed Military and civilians poured in. Out of the scores of testimonials received by the family of PVC Shaitan Singh I will like to quote one by Lt. Gen. Bikram Singh, GOC, who wrote,

My dear Suraj Bhan Singhji,

I am really proud that I had an officer like late Major Shaitan Singh under my command both here and in Naga Hills. I had the highest regard for him ever since I came in close touch with him and there was no doubt in my mind that he had all the qualities of a perfect gentleman and a brave soldier and that one day he was sure to make a name for himself and his family. Though Major. Shaitan Singh is no more in this world but he has made himself immortal by his supreme sacrifice for the cause of our motherland. Needless to say that the future progeny will always remember with reverence people like Major Shaitan Singh who never hesitated to pay the highest price in keeping the hard won freedom of the country. I would like to congratulate you and the family for producing such an outstanding soldier. It is not only the Army but the whole country is indebted to him. . . .

Yours sincerely,

Sd. Bikram Singh *(Rastraveer Major Shaitan Singh Smriti Granth,* p.64.*)*

**The Collapse of Top Leadership**

Lieutenant General (Retd.) VK Singh PVSM, writes in his article *Winds of War - the 1962 and 1985 Conflict,* in the book *The Indian Army: A Brief History*, says candidly,

"There has been a criminal neglect of the Army's modernisation. All its equipment was of World War II vintage. As a result, the Indian Army was outgunned and outclassed by the enemy.

"When actual fighting started, much of the leadership from the Brigade and above was found wanting, unable to take quick decisions and prone to succumb to their fears.

"Nevertheless, at battalion, company and junior level, the Indian Army fought with its usual courage, fortitude and willingness to sacrifice their lives, if needed. Time and time again, units and subunits, cut off, faced by superior enemy forces had fought on, often to the last man and last round. It was this realisation that the core values of the Army were still intact that gave hope that the spirit of the Army could be quickly revived." (*The Indian Army: A Brief History*, pp.108-109.)

**Good out of Bad**

Out of 24,000 of all ranks, who participated in this war, 1423 jawans, JCOs and officers of Indian Army were killed, 3018 were wounded and 3587 taken prisoner. Also 1655 personnel were missing, and it was presumed that they were killed.

But nothing is entirely useless. The 1962 War, so ignobly lost, was not a total loss. Though we lost face and were humbled, yet a lesson was learnt. The eyes of the Government of India were opened. Prime Minister Nehru was jerked out of his ideal dream world. The chief actors of this rout, Defense Minister Krishna Menon, Chief of Army Staff General Thapar and the inapt General Kaul resigned. Shri YB Chavan took over as Defense Minister and appointed Lt. General JN

Chaudhuri as Chief of Army Staff. The Government recognised the need to modernise the Army and expand it to face threat of Pakistan and China simultaneously. Six new divisions were planned. Some of the new and old divisions were especially trained in mountain warfare, with the result that now India has one of the best mountain warfare forces in the world.

To increase the number of officers emergency commissions were given and to train these officers new Officers' Training Schools were opened at Madras and Pune. And this happened just at the correct time, because in 1965 Pakistan invaded India and then Indian Army stood vindicated and victorious.

*Shaitan Singh Nagar Railway Station*

## Homage to PVC Major Shaitan Singh

I am a flame,
A red hot ember,
Of love and honour.
Name or fame, I do not crave,
I live, only to serve Mother India
I live, only to save my country —
For that I will sacrifice my life,
Always and ever.
From battle to turn back? Never.
Bullets or bombs can burn my flesh,
Yet, my resolution will never waver.
A hundred pieces of shrapnel
May pierce my body, lacerate my heart,
My blood may flow and my organs may fall,
And my eyes pop out of their sockets,
And my intestines spill out, yet
Till I have breath, I will fight,
With my blood, I will pay
My oblation to the Gods of India,
I will crimson with my blood,
The snows of Regang La.
As a soldier true and proud,
I will die, for I am
A flame of sacrifice
I, Major Shaitan Singh
Of Charlie Company.

# Colonel Dhan Singh Thapa

## 10 April 1928 - 5 September 2005

### Birth and Childhood

On 10 April 1928, a son was born to Shri Prem Singh Thapa and Mrs Draupadi Thapa at the beautiful hill station Shimla in Himachal Pradesh. The fond parents, even in their wildest dreams, had not imagined that one day their beloved eldest son would become one of the 21 bravest soldiers of India to be awarded India's highest battle honour, the Param Vir Chakra. Later three more sons, and the last, a daughter, were born to the couple.

Shri Prem Singh worked in a goldsmith's shop in Solan as a skilled worker. When Dhan Singh was 12, Prem Singh moved to Shimla because most of their relatives lived there and he thought it would be good for the children to be with their uncles, aunts and cousins. However, he had to struggle to re-establish himself in this new place and started a small business there, but somehow it didn't do too well. Then he fell ill and died.

It was a shattering blow for Draupdi who was left with five young children and hardly any means of livelihood. The responsibility of bringing up and educating five children fell on the shoulders of young Dhan Singh and his mother. In India, family values were strong then. They moved into the house of Dhan Singh's maternal uncle. Unfortunately, his uncle was a man of modest means and also had six children of his own. Those were days of extreme poverty and privation. Existence itself became a struggle. Cramped in a small house, each day was a battle to feed and educate the eleven children.

Adversity disheartens and defeats most people, but some exceptional ones become stronger on the anvil of misfortune; the greater the adversity, the greater becomes the resolve of these rare brave souls. While facing overwhelming odds, their inner fire burns up all the weaknesses of their nature and they come out of their ordeal as unalloyed steel. Young Dhan Singh was one such person. He decided that life has to be lived as it comes; it is no use bemoaning our bad-luck. He took all the trials in his stride.

Dhan Singh was obsessed with education and was convinced that education was the road leading to a better quality of life and he wanted to do his best to give his family a better life. To achieve his objective, he was ready to undergo any hardship, undertake any task. He studied in Gorkha School and at the same time took up a part-time job to earn something to meet the expenses of his family, and to take care of the education of his siblings. He had to walk about 20 km daily in the hilly terrain of Shimla to attend school and to do his part-time job. He kept smiling at life with the conviction that one day life would smile back at him.

Even in his early teens Dhan Singh had a heightened sense of duty, responsibility and self-respect. His motto was that a man's hand should always be stretched out to give and not to beg. He gave a large portion of his earnings to his uncle. He himself helped with the household chores so that his uncle and aunt would not feel them to be a burden and also ensured that his brothers helped to the best of their ability. However, he felt sad when he saw his beloved young sister doing heavy household chores. She being the youngest, he was very protective about her.

His one hobby was playing football. Whenever he could, he played football with his school mates. He always maintained that he learnt team spirit by playing football in his Gorkha School. Despite the grim struggle and many difficulties he had to face while staying with his maternal uncle, he understood the situation of his uncle and was grateful to him for the shelter and support his family received from him.

## True Patriot: Refuses a Job in London

With all the household work and his part-time job, it was very difficult for Dhan Singh to pass his high school examination. But by dint of hard work he not only passed his matriculation exams but in addition, he managed to learn good English from an English lady living in Shimla, for whom he worked as an assistant. This lady was so impressed by Dhan Singh's efficiency, integrity and endeavours to improve himself that she constantly encouraged him and also taught him etiquette. When she left for England, she offered him a job in London. Even today many educated and uneducated youth of India try hard to secure a job abroad. They take the best from Mother India and then go and serve in foreign lands. But though poor, Dhan Singh was a staunch patriot. He rejected this tempting job offer, which could have lifted him out of poverty and taken him to the fabled city of London. He was not willing to leave his country.

## Dream Fulfilled: Selected in the Army

After passing his matriculation examinations, Dhan Singh began to work in a bank. On a fateful day someone suggested to him that he ought to join the Army. It was as if this person had spelled out his own dream. This is what he had dreamt and aspired for in the hidden recesses of his heart. The Army was his true vocation. But the family was so hard up that after matriculation he had to take whatever job was available. By this time his younger brothers were grown up. Now his heart took wings. He decided to join the Army and set off to find out how he could get into the Army. He decided that once settled in the Army, he would bring his family to live with him.

He was thrilled when he got selected for the Army. He was commissioned into the 1st Battalion of the 8th Gorkha Rifles on 28 August 1949, at the age of 21. He became popular because he had a cheerful disposition and was a good sportsman and a great team player. Fierce bravery, total loyalty, dedication and discipline are inborn in Gorkhas. Dhan Singh had an additional advantage that he spoke Gorkhali, therefore his men of the 8th Gorkha Rifles could relate to him easily. As an officer, his first concern was to ensure the comfort of his men. He always led by example and was both loyal and respectful, which made him respected by his men and even his seniors relied on him. Dhan Singh was a very lively and adventurous person who believed in living life to the fullest. He had not let his childhood struggles scar him in anyway. He was positive and full of life and raring to go. During his bachelor days he had bought a horse and cut a dashing figure when he was out riding. Later, he and some of his fellow officers bought a jeep by pooling their resources, and went on picnics to far flung places, where they lit bonfires and enjoyed themselves.

## A True Leader

Apart from courage, fearlessness, loyalty and tenacity, Dhan Singh had also developed leadership qualities. He believed that an Army Officer had an opportunity to become a true leader of men. Dhan Singh cared more for his soldiers than for his superiors. He was convinced that an officer has to be a role model for his followers. He should himself have the qualities which he would like them to acquire. Men would never follow a man whom they cannot trust. He said, "The morale of a company depends upon the morale of its leader. The officer should be the first to undertake a dangerous mission. If you have a rotten company, then surely you are a rotten officer." He was always well-groomed, his uniform spotless and starched because he had the conviction, "An officer has to respect his uniform. An officer wearing a spotted uniform and stubble cannot feel dignified." His life's two formulas were:

1. Conviction backed by Determination leads to Realisation.

2. Determination leads first to Small and then to Big Successes.

## Marriage

As soon as Dhan Singh was commissioned in the Army, his mother began to pester him to get married. Dhan Singh wanted to serve in the Army with total dedication, without any distractions. But in 1955, his mother and family, through their emotional appeals or rather emotional blackmail, persuaded him to marry.

In the beginning, his young and beautiful wife Shukla found it hard to adjust to postings to places like Jammu and Nagaland but when she observed the intense enthusiasm and enjoyment of her husband while on duty or with his soldiers, she too fell in love with the adventurous life of the Army.

## In Nagaland

On 29 September 1956, Dhan Singh got his permanent regular commission. He was posted to Mokokchung in Nagaland. At the time of his posting there, Nagaland was in turmoil; separatists were revolting against Nagaland being included in India and there were intense anti-government activities. The Army was sent to take control of the situation. The Naga ethnic groups were terrorising the local villagers. The hostiles were always ready to ambush whenever and wherever they felt threatened. The morale of the hostiles was high as they had been successful in some of their ambushes. 1956 to 1962 was a particularly difficult period in Naga Hills as in those days our Army lacked the experience of countering insurgency and was also short of equipment, vehicles and wireless communication equipment. Added to these were the difficult terrain and harsh weather in this strategically important part of India. As this region is covered with dense forests and is close to China, Burma and East Pakistan, any discontent was bound to be exploited by China and Pakistan. It was a time of continuous patrolling, innumerable raids, ambushes and searches carried out by officers, junior commissioned officers and soldiers of the Indian Army.

The 1/8 Gorkha Rifles had a tough time persuading the villagers to cooperate with the security forces, but without their cooperation controlling the insurgency would have been still more difficult. Captain Dhan Singh was a born conciliator. With his philosophical approach and sense of humour, he soon developed friendly relations with the Naga villagers. Whenever possible, he mediated between the Army and the locals, as he was respected by both.

During operations in Nagaland, Shukla, who was expecting their second child, was left alone with her daughter, while her husband went for night-patrolling. Even when Shukla gave birth to her second daughter, Dhan Singh was out on night patrol against the insurgents. Shukla had only the midwife to help her but she took it in her stride. She knew how happy her husband was while fighting for his country. She tried never to bother him with her problems, never told him about the fear she felt at night when he was out to ambush the insurgents.

Dhan Singh maintained that his work in Nagaland, though dangerous, helped him a lot during the Chinese War and during his time as a Chinese prisoner, psychologically and strategically.

## Two Angelic Daughters

Dhanu (as Dhan Singh was fondly called) and Shukla had two daughters, on whom they doted. Dhan Singh felt that his daughters were God's most wonderful gift to him. He was a family man and he considered his unit as his first family and his actual family came second. Whenever in command of a unit, he organised picnics for the families of soldiers, seeking to bond them through enjoyment in a relaxed atmosphere. He enjoyed immensely the Dushera celebrations held on a grand scale by his Gorkha Unit. He took pains to make the occasion especially memorable for his officers and troops.

*Area of Pangong Tso where he was posted in 1962*

## July 1962: Posting to Chushul

In August 1962 Dhan Singh came home on leave. The house was full of his love and laughter. Shukla was expecting their third child and hoped that this time when the delivery took place he would be home as he was not due for field posting. Suddenly the battlefield called him and the Gods of valour chose to test him.

Shukla was upset by his sudden departure but Dhan Singh prophetically assured her, "Don't worry. I will get a medal and you will come with me to receive the honour."

In July 1962, while outwardly chanting the mantra "Hindi Chini Bhai-Bhai", the deceitful Chinese were preparing a full-fledged attack on India. And we gullible Indians, led by an idealistic and most naive Prime Minister also chanted in tune, "Hindi Chini Bhai-Bhai".

Even though Sardar Vallabhbhai Patel had in a letter to Prime Minister Jawahar Lal Nehru, detailed the dangers from China, Jawahar Lal chose to ignore him. He also rejected a defence plan made by General Thorat for the defence of Ladhak and NEFA. Having neglected and undermined the Army for nearly two decades after Independence, he gave it an impossible task. He chose to walk on the precipice, provoking China by accepting the advice of a civilian Intelligence

Chief and asked the Army to establish small posts opposite the posts established by China, going against the advice of his own Army Chief, General Thimmaya. The Army commanders pointed out that these posts would be almost impossible to defend, as there were no roads to supply them food, arms or ammunition, while the Chinese had a superb infrastructure and could supply their troops with all they needed. But our Prime Minister overlooked the harsh realities.

## The Battle of Sirijap: 30 "Fearless" Gorkhas

Field Marshal Sam Manekshaw has said, "*Anyone who says he is totally fearless is either a liar or a Gorkha.*" How true this is will be shown by the following account of the battle of Sirijap, where 30 ill-equipped, half-fed brave hearts mowed down and chopped off the heads of 150 fully armed, well fed and well clad soldiers of Chinese Army.

The battle of Sirijap should be written in letters of gold in the history of the Indian Army, a bright page in the dark defeat of that inglorious war with China. How did it happen? Who was responsible for this dark chapter in the history of Indian Army? One can say with absolute conviction that it was not the fault of the Armed Forces but of our political leadership.

Captain Dhan Singh was posted to Chusul. He was the commanding officer of 'D' Company of Gorkha Battalion and was asked to establish a forward post at Sirijap. In those days the Indian Army was not equipped to fight at such heights. Some of the soldiers didn't even have proper boots. Dhan Singh was asked to do the suicidal, the impossible. He knew the risks, yet in the best army tradition, he undertook the task allotted to him. The 'D' Company was made responsible for the construction of defences in 30 sq. miles of the area.

In September and November 1962 the Chinese and the Indians were trying to control the area between Pangong Lake and Spanggur Lake. India was establishing forward posts under the mistaken belief that China would never attack the Indian Army. On account of the number of small posts to be established all over, only 30 men of 'D' Company were available for the defence of Sirijap 1; the second post was established on the banks of the Yula. On 22 September the Chinese occupied ground halfway between Sirijap 1 & 2. Sirijap 1 Post was brought up to platoon strength (a platoon has 30 to 36 soldiers) approximately by the end of September 1962.

The Chinese military strategy was to attack our scattered newly established posts in large numbers with tanks and artillery support and force the small Indian garrisons with insufficient manpower of 20 to 30 soldiers, either to evacuate or fight it out to the tragic end.

**"The Indian Army Needs Almost Everything Except Courage"**

While reporting on the Sino-Indian War the American magazine *Time* summed up the situation of Indian Army thus: "The Indian Army needs almost everything except courage." The following narrative highlights the heights of courage on one front of the War.

## First Attack

On 19 October, there was a dramatic increase in the Chinese complement around Sirijap 1, with the arrival of a large contingent of enemy troops along with heavy guns and infantry support weapons. This was a clear indication that an attack on Sirijap was imminent. Captain Dhan Singh asked his soldiers to dig deep and fast to protect the post. But digging in that frosted ground was not easy.

The soaring, 6,000m high mountains, bone-piercing winds and sub-zero temperatures made survival difficult for our ill-prepared troops. Even for their sustenance, they depended on supplies by air or by ferry. It made them extremely vulnerable in case of an attack. But having lived a rough and tough life in hilly areas and being used to that harsh climate, though nowhere as harsh as at Sirijap, the Gorkhas could offer stout resistance.

The Chinese launched their first attack on Sirijap Post on 20 October 1962 at 4.30. They surrounded the Post in overwhelming numbers on three sides from the rear. Covered and supported by heavy artillery and mortar fire the Chinese advanced up to 150 yards to the rear of the post. About 600 Chinese were advancing, confident of making short work of the Indian soldiers. They didn't know what veritable war gods were these handful of Gorkha soldiers. When the Chinese were about 150 yards away, the Gorkhas of Sirijap1 broke like 30 Furies on the Chinese with their light machine guns and rifles and killed and wounded large numbers of them. Such was the fierceness of their attack that the Chinese were stopped at a distance of 100 yards from the post.

But 'D' company had to pay a heavy price too. Many of our valiant Gorkhas died or were wounded. Naik Krishnabahadur Thapa was badly wounded yet took charge of a light machine gun after its crew was killed and in spite of blood pouring out from his many wounds kept on firing till he was killed. To make the situation worse, during the attack our troops' land communication link with the battalion was destroyed.

## Second Attack

Captain Dhan Singh Thapa encouraged his soldiers and made preparations to face the next attack, which they knew they would have to face. For their second attack the Chinese intensified their artillery fire and under its cover advanced up to 50 yards from the post. They threw incendiary bombs at the post hoping to burn it. Sensing that the situation was hopeless Captain Dhan Singh told his troops, "We will take bullets on our chests, never on our backs." and shouting the famous Gorkha battle cry, "Ayo Gorkhali" he and his troops fired at the advancing Chinese. He became a veritable god of Death and began to shoot at the advancing Chinese soldiers. He and his second-in-command Subedar Min Bahadur Gurung went from post to post to encourage and help the remaining soldiers.

With hand grenades and small arms, the incredible Gorkhas beat back the second attack too. Subedar Min Bahadur Singh was buried under the debris of his collapsed bunker, but he came out from under the debris and lifting his LMG shot dozens of the advancing Chinese, till he himself was killed. But for the time being the second Chinese attack too was repulsed.

## The Third Attack

23 brave Indians were martyred on those icy heights in these two attacks. They washed the sacred Motherland with their blood. Now only seven of the gallant defenders were alive. But the remaining seven were not disheartened; they were as if doubly charged with patriotism and valour, ready to die but not without killing ten times more of the enemy.

For their third attack the Chinese brought tanks, heavy machine guns, bazookas and four amphibian crafts, each armed with two heavy machine guns. As mentioned earlier the communication links of 'D' company with the battalion headquarters had been destroyed. The battalion headquarters, situated on the other shore of the lake, sent Naik Rabilal Thapa in a small boat to find out what was happening at Sirijap and if possible to help the 'D' company. Another boat came from Tokung. The Chinese spotted the boats and brought heavy fire upon them. One of the boats sank taking all the occupants to an icy grave. But Naik Rabilal Thapa escaped.

The advancing Chinese lobbed an incendiary bomb on the bunker of Captain Dhan Singh Thapa. As their ammunition was exhausted, the seven surviving Gorkhas came out of their trenches. Then began a fierce hand to hand fight. Brandishing their shining and sharp Khukhris the awesome Gorkhas attacked the Chinese like live thunderbolts. The Chinese were taken aback as they had thought that these handful of men would be easy prey and they would surrender in the first attack. But inspired by the bravery of their leader Dhan Singh the Gorkha soldiers fought against heavy odds, without wavering, till they died. Out of the seven surviving defenders of Sirijap, four died in the third Chinese attack.

One Chinese soldier, who had no bullets left in his rifle, saw Captain Dhan Singh charging at him with his blood smeared Khukri. He lifted his rifle butt to hit Dhan Singh but he twisted his face away and the butt hit his teeth and he lost his two front teeth. Unmindful of his injury Dhan Singh slashed the Chinese with his Khukri and felled him down. (Later Dhan Singh, who looked for the silver lining in every situation, would joke that his two false front teeth were "magical teeth" because he could make them appear and disappear at will.)

The advancing Chinese lobbed another incendiary bomb on the bunker of Captain Dhan Singh Thapa. While he was extinguishing the fire caused by this incendiary grenade by rolling over it, the Chinese, who by this time had overrun his post, overpowered him. He and the other prisoners were marched off to Khurnak Fort and subsequently sent to Sinkiang, as Prisoners of War. Surely Mother Durga had put an invisible and invincible armour around Dhan Singh, otherwise with shells raining all around, the Chinese charging, the tanks advancing, how could a person rolling on a burning grenade escape death?

Seeing the Sirijap Post burning, Naik Rabilal Thapa reported to the Headquarters that Sirijap was captured and all the soldiers of 'D' Company were killed. Captain Dhan Singh Thapa was promoted as Major and awarded a posthumous Param Vir Chakra.

## The Three Survivors

Actually, three of 'D' company had survived. The battalion came to know much later that Major Dhan Singh Thapa and another soldier had been taken prisoners. The third survivor, Rifleman Tulsi Ram Thapa, escaped and after hoodwinking the Chinese for four days, rejoined his battalion. (Gen. VK Singh PVSM, in his article *Winds of War - the 1962 and 1985 Conflict,* in the book *The Indian Army: A Brief History* says there were seven survivors, while Gen. Cardozo writes there were only two survivors) After repatriation Major Dhan Singh's co-prisoner narrated an incident, "Major Dhan Singh was manning the light machine gun of his unit when he saw one of his soldiers shot in the arm. The gun fell down beyond the soldier's reach and then there was silence from that quarter. In the dense smoke-covered air, unmindful of the shells falling all around, Dhan Singh ran to the soldier's trench, picked up his rifle and tapping the crouching soldier, gave him his gun and said in Gorkhali, '*Kafur hunu bhanda marnu niko.*' i.e. 'It is better to die than to be a coward!' Then he ran back to man the LMG as the gunner had been shot dead."

## The Battle Lost: Undefeated

Dhan Singh and his gallant men had held at bay more than 500 Chinese in which only 3 men of 1/8 Gorkhas survived but the Chinese suffered more than 150 casualties. The 1962 war really pained Dhan Singh that despite doing their best in the harshest of circumstances and despite the sacrifice of so many lives of his beloved soldiers, they lost the war.

After capturing Sirijap 1, the Chinese turned their attention to Sirijap 2, and captured it, only after very stiff resistance. Very few came out alive from this battle. Those that did, spoke of the cruel Chinese lining up the Indian wounded and shooting them dead.

Sometimes victory is defeat and defeat is victory. For India, there was one solace even in defeat, with so many sons of India displaying not just bravery but incredible courage in the face of huge numbers of enemy, armed with tanks and heavy machine guns, in that sub zero temperature. It was a war which revealed rare heroism.

And let us be clear on one point; this was not a defeat of the Indian Army because only 24,000 Indian military personnel out of 30 lakhs participated in this battle. It was a defeat of an ignorant, misguided gullible and unrealistically idealistic civilian leadership, which was assisted in this downfall by some "Yes Men" of the higher Army hierarchy who did not oppose the foolhardy venture and above all, the wrong advice of our security agencies. (See Endnote)

## Declared Dead

In 1962 television had not yet made in-roads into our lives. The only source of news was the radio. Like the wives of all those who were fighting at the front, Shukla, who was seven months pregnant, tried to listen to radio news, as much as she could, in the hope of getting some information about her husband. Visualising her husband in that freezing cold, she was knitting a pullover for him, which she planned to present to him on his return. She switched from one news channel to another trying to get more news. One day she heard on a Punjabi Channel, "Major Dhan Singh is declared dead." Since the news was in Punjabi, which she didn't know and since Dhan Singh had been a captain when he left for war (she was unaware that he had been promoted to the rank of Major during the war), she told her mother-in-law, "How sad. Poor Major and his family. His wife must be devastated", without realising that she was the wife. Her family was in a dilemma about how to give her the cruel news, since she was facing a tough pregnancy, apart from the tremendous stress of her husband fighting in the War.

## "My Husband is Alive"

When the family received the official telegram of Major Dhan Singh's death in action they were forced to inform her. Upon hearing the devastating news, Shukla went into a state of shock. But, strangely contradicting the "news" deep down in her heart, she believed that one day her husband would return to her. So every evening, following her usual routine, she would sit in her pooja room with her daughters and do pooja. Her faith in God wasn't shaken, she didn't ask HIM "why" or "why me?" but with quiet trust, went on in her belief in God.

Lt. Col. J.D. Karwal sent a letter of condolence to Mrs. Shukla Thapa on 27 October 1962. Gen. P.N. Thapar sent a letter of condolence to her on 28 December 1962.

Due to the pressure of an orthodox society, Shukla had to undergo the rites of widowhood. She had to wear a white sari and had to stop wearing sindoor. This really depressed her as she had the faith that "Dhan Singh Will Return." Some ignorant and ill-willed people, instead of sympathising with her, taunted her that the child in her womb was "ill-fated (*manhoos*)" and "was responsible for the death of his father (*apne baap ko kha gaya*)." Rooted in her faith that her husband was alive and in course of time would return home, Shukla didn't break down. She had tremendous faith in God. Standing firm in her faith, she also gave strength to her mother, father, brother and her mother-in-law. Shukla's mother was deeply religious. She kept the telegram announcing Dhan Singh's death in her pooja room on a pedestal in front of the idol. One day, when she opened her eyes after her meditation, she found the telegram lying on the floor, even though there had been no wind and nobody had entered the room. This incident strengthened Shukla's belief that her husband was alive.

## A Prisoner

Major Dhan Singh had a living faith in God. When he was taken prisoner and kept in isolation, he found a black oval stone with a half white circle on one end which seemed to him like a Shivling. He prayed to it. Once a Chinese interrogator asked him "Do you believe in God?" He looked the interrogator straight in the eyes and answered firmly, "Yes, definitely." The Chinese said, "Prove it!" He told the Chinese, "Whom God saves, nobody can kill. (*Jako Rakhe Saiyan Maar Sake na Koi*) I survived the battle against all odds. I could have been killed but despite your worst efforts, I didn't die, because of my God who didn't want me to die. This is nothing short of a miracle."

The Chinese wasn't convinced. Then Dhan Singh opened his jacket and said, "You have your gun, shoot and kill me if you can. It is my belief that you could not kill me in the battle and you will not be able to kill me now because my God doesn't want me to die." Disconcerted by the ferocious intensity in Dhan Singh's eyes, the Chinese soldier moved on to interrogate another officer. The Chinese were especially harsh towards Major Dhan Singh Thapa because in spite of their best efforts he refused to make any statement against the Indian Government.

The Chinese used to taunt the Indian prisoners, "We have informed your Government about your existence but they are not interested in you at all. You are unwanted by your Government." They wanted them to believe that they were abandoned by their country and Government.

## Cultivates one of the Captors

During the seven months as prisoner of war, Major Dhan Singh was put in solitary confinement and was forced to remain awake up to 48 hours at a stretch. The Chinese broke all military conventions and inflicted a series of inhuman punishments on Indian prisoners. Due to being kept in freezing cold and being made to walk in the snow without proper shoes, Major Dhan Singh suffered from frostbite, and developed arthritis and high blood pressure. Thereafter, he had to bid a final goodbye to his passion for playing football.

While interned in the Chinese isolation camp, Major Dhan Singh spent his time praying to the Shivling to grant him the needed peace and strength of mind. On 26 October 1962 he wrote a letter to his family but the problem was how to send it! He had a talent for making friends. As mentioned before, in Nagaland he had honed his skills of how to make friends of enemies by treating them with positivity and cheerfulness. Here he made friends with a small boy who used to bring him his food. Talking in sign language he began to cultivate him. He asked the boy to teach him how to eat with chopsticks. The boy felt important that he was teaching an officer the Chinese way of eating.

One day Dhan Singh asked him to post a letter to his uncle in Shimla. Dhan Singh managed to convey to him by sign language that his wife was pregnant and must be suffering a lot. The letter would relieve her mind. The boy had become fond of Dhan Singh and posted the letter. Thus the letter reached Dhan Singh's house on 30 December 1962 with the information that he was alive and a prisoner-of-war.

On 4 January 1963 Dhan Singh's brother-in-law sent a letter to the Chief of Army Staff that Dhan Singh's uncle in Shimla had received a letter from him on 30 December 1962. On the same day, Dhan Singh's brother-in-law Man Bahadur Thapa received confirmation from the government that Dhan Singh was alive and a prisoner of war. By 5 January 1963 the media splashed the news all over the country.

Once the news reached Shukla, she was too happy to reproach those who had taunted her that the child in her womb was ill-fated. Now the same people, who had held her unborn son responsible for the death of his father, did a complete U-turn and declared, "He is such a lucky child; he pulled his father out of the death well". After seven months in captivity Dhan Singh was released by the Chinese. He came home and held his son in his arms, a son who would later follow in the illustrious footsteps of his father. He named his son Paramdeep.

## Param Vir Chakra

Major Dhan Singh Thapa was honoured with the Param Vir Chakra medal on 26 January 1964. Thus he fulfilled the prophetic promise he had made to his wife Shukla upon being posted to Chusul, "Don't worry. I will get a medal and you will come with me to receive the honour." He won not just any medal, but the highest honour of Indian Army.

Dhan Singh believed that heroism was not the prerogative of only those who get a medal, there were others too who displayed great bravery and initiative on the battlefield yet missed the medals.

## Citation

### Major Dhan Singh Thapa

### 1/8 Gorkha Rifles (IC 7990)

Major Dhan Singh Thapa was in command of a forward post in Ladakh. On 20 October it was attacked by the Chinese in overwhelming strength after being subjected to intensive artillery and mortar bombardment. Under his gallant command, the greatly outnumbered post repulsed the attack, inflicting heavy casualties on the aggressors. The enemy attacked again in greater numbers after heavy shelling by artillery and mortar fire. Under the leadership of Major Thapa, his men repulsed this attack also with heavy losses to the enemy.

The Chinese attacked for the third time, now with tanks to support their infantry. The post had already suffered large numbers of casualties in the earlier two attacks. Though considerably reduced in number it held out to the last. When it was finally overrun by overwhelming numbers of the enemy, Major Thapa got out of his trench and killed several of the enemy in hand-to-hand fighting before he was finally overpowered by Chinese soldiers.

Major Thapa's cool courage, conspicuous fighting qualities and leadership were in the highest traditions of our Army.

Gazette of India Notification

No. 68 – Press/62

*Receiving PVC from the President*

**The Dashing Hero** (Reminiscences of Lt. Col. A K Sharma (Retd.)

With the highest battle honour of India on his breast, PVC Dhan Singh Thapa was in his element. Lt. Col. A K Sharma (Retd.) remembers him thus:

"My best memories of him are of 1963 vintage, from our days as Gentlemen Cadets (GCs) in the Indian Military Academy (IMA). He used to be beardless, like most Gorkhas, then. He was invariably splendidly resplendent in his uniform and cut a fine figure in the Shining Eighth's Olive Greens, black leather Sam Browne, black lanyard, red shoulder flashes with jet black mini-regimental crests, and in a very rakishly tilted Gorkha Hat with the bright red plume brush of a Scottish Highland Regiment – The Black Watch – that the 8 Gorkha Rifles had a battle-association within the Great War. And, to boot, he used to sport the coveted purple 'ribbonned' Param Vir Chakra (PVC) on his left breast. It was bestowed on him posthumously! Yes, posthumously, because he had been declared 'missing believed dead' in October 1962 during India's China war. He was reported as having perished whilst defending the Sirijap post on the Pangong Tso on 21 October 1962. When he showed up back in Dehradun one afternoon in 1963, all were overjoyed, including his 'widow', who was married to him again, just to be on the right side of the Hindu holy trinity!

"We heard on the radio and read in the papers, that the jawans had fought very bravely in Rezang La and Spanggur Lake gap in Ladakh, and at Walong in NEFA. Amongst the GCs fraternity, there was talk of Dhan Singh Thapa, the war-hero, in person, having been posted to the IMA. What a big morale booster it was for us to see him amidst us one fine day!

"He became a role model for me and was the motivation for me to opt for the Gorkhas, despite being a 'tech' from the National Defense Academy. For our lot of Gentlemen Cadets (GCs) of Bravo Battalion of the IMA, Maj Dhan Singh Thapa was inspiration personified for equalling, if not surpassing the Chinese in fighting. He was playful, approachable, always smiling, and very off-hand about his gallantry award. I've known him to be a simple person right down to his ammunition boots, but large hearted, as all Gorkha soldiers tend to be. Much in the mould of a simple infanteer that he was, he also displayed in ample measure, the good military mettle of duty, honour, discipline, dedication, loyalty and integrity, which were inborn in him. He was neither the charismatic leader, nor the agro-warrior. He was, in fact, the type that did his duty quietly, willingly, efficiently and without fuss or fuming. Like other war heroes I've known, he was also a great one who would think nothing of making light of his PVC; for example, he recounted to our platoon that he got it for just throwing back at the assaulting Chinese, the stick-hand grenades, that, they kept lobbing into his post, the whole day! Who says that old guts and gore doesn't have a funny face?

"I have had the honour of being trained personally by Maj Dhan Singh Thapa who was an umpire over me in the final mountain warfare camp on the Bhadraj feature, the western-most crest in the skyline on the Mussorie Hills range. Catching me unshaven on parade, he once ran after me with a drawn khukri to administer a close shave without the essential comforts of either hot water or of shaving lather! He would often turn up at night in front of our defence works and

***With his unit Gorkhas***

lob boulders amongst us with the accompanying picture-painting cries of "Ennemmy shellinggg cumminng! Ennemmy shellinngg cummingg"! Some boulders hurt, indeed, but they did bring home the essential lesson of the danger and fog of war, along with this dry battle inoculation, of course!

"He had been posted to the Indian Military Academy straight after his incarceration as a Prisoner Of War in Sinkiang. The Chinese could not break him, despite the third degree torture, privations and the 'brain-washing'. Against all norms of soldierly conduct, he was punished severely for inflicting very heavy casualties on Chinese assaulting his position, and for his stubborn refusal in making disparaging signed written statements against the Indian Army and the Indian government. The Chinese political officers at that time were trying all sorts of tricks to force the Gorkha troops to make anti-India statements. In all exuberance and innocence, when asked, by our lot of the GCs as to how they 'brain-washed' him, he retorted with a straight face 'They just took it out, and washed it in ice cold water!' "

## Republic Day Parade

After receiving the Param Vir Chakra in 1964, till his death, PVC Dhan Singh Thapa, except for once, never missed any Republic Day Parade, not even when he had severe medical problems. He had arthritis and his foot got swollen due to standing in his jeep for hours throughout the parade. He felt that he was a representative of all the brave soldiers of the Indian Army and took the salute on their behalf. In fact at the age of 74, suffering from kidney failure, due to which he would faint suddenly, he still went for his last Republic Day Parade on 26 January, 2003. He was an Army man to the last. Even after retirement, he never refused any invitation to any Army event. He used to love being with soldiers.

## 1971 War with Pakistan

During the 1971 War with Pakistan Major Dhan Singh was posted to Gurez as Commanding Officer of 1 JAK LI. He commanded the

1 JAK LI from September 1971 to February 1974. It was a time of continuous patrolling, innumerable raids, ambushes and searches carried out by officers, JCOs and soldiers.

After the War, he got posted to places like Ambala, Jallandhar, and Devlali.

## Retirement

Dhan Singh retired on 30 April 1980 and then at that advanced age was re-employed up to December 1982 in Sikkim Transit Camp, away from his family and again in mountains.

## After Retirement

After retirement Col. Dhan Singh worked in Udaipur for a marble company and then in Vapi for a phosphorous company. One day Sri Subroto Roy of Sahara Pariwar, who is a great fan of Indian Armed Forces called him for inauguration of his command office and thus started a relationship with Sahara India Pariwar which continued till his last breath and still continues as Sahara India Pariwar gives his wife Shukla Thapa the same regards and honour which they gave to her husband.

## Awards / Decorations

Param Vir Chakra - 1962 War

GS Medal - "Naga Hills"

Saina Seva Medal - "Himalaya"

Clasp Ladakh to GS Medal - 1947

Raksha Medal - 1965

## Education Forever

PVC Dhan Singh continued his education and even passed his MBA after his retirement. He kept taking some correspondence course or other. His long term retirement plan was to open a school for children in his village and provide good education to them. He even bought some land in Dehradun with his little savings and by selling his wife's jewellery for this dream school for the village children. However, due to certain family circumstances, he gave away this land to his brothers for their livelihood. He died of kidney failure, from which he had suffered for one and a half years, on 5 September 2005, aged 75. Even when he was admitted to hospital for two months, whenever a doctor, nurse or guest came to visit him and asked him about his health, he invariably replied with a twinkle and thumbs up sign "Absolutely fit and fine." He never deviated from that reply till his last breath and went to the Lord with a smile on his face. Even though his kidneys failed, his indomitable will never sagged. It is significant that he should have died on Teachers Day, he who placed education next to patriotism.

When will we Indians realise that while we glamorise film stars, cricketers or even politicians, we ignore our war heroes, most of them unsung and unwept for, but without whom India might be again enslaved!

## Family

Col. Dhan Singh had four children - 3 daughters and one son. He gave the best possible education to his children, as education had always been his priority in life. He was a great advocate of women's education and believed they should become independent. Therefore, his three daughters were well educated and are working. He believed "All Indians Are equal". He never had any problem when his children married out of caste. His eldest daughter Pamela is married to Col Ranbir Chauhan (Retd.) and manages an Eco Friendly Shop in the Park Hotel, Delhi. The second daughter Madhulika Monga is married to Mr. Aman Monga and works with Sahara India Television, Pune. His son Col. Paramdeep Thapa is married to Ms. Anushree Chouba. He joined the same unit in which his father worked. After retirement he is working in DLF Company in Delhi as Chief Security Officer, DLF, Pan India.

## Second Marriage

Col. Thapa's second marriage to his first wife is a good example of the irrationality of some of our religious beliefs. When Maj. Dhan Singh Thapa was declared dead, all the rites for the dead and his widow were completed. However, after he returned from China, the rites of his being born were held and he was remarried to Shukla. After their second marriage, their youngest daughter Poornima was born. Ms. Poornima Thapa is living with her mother Mrs. Shukla Thapa and works with Aamby Valley Ltd. in Pune.

### A Level Playing Field

My life willingly will I offer

At Mother India's altar,

Not an inch of our Motherland will I cede.

But one thing I ask

Before my heart stops

To beat. I supplicate,

Give us a level playing field,

Give us a fighting chance.

Do not send us to war

Without a strategy,

Without a clear appraisal

Of the enemy's strength.

Let our death not be in vain,

Let not our blood flow down the drain.

We are your brothers and sons

Your very own.

Do not send us to war,

With obsolete arms,
With uniforms
Unable to keep out
The bone-piercing winds,
With shoes too loose or tight.
Give us enough food,
To give us full strength
To carry our guns and backpacks
And struggle over mule tracks
Where there is no toe-hold.
O my countrymen!
Give us a level playing field.
Adequate arms,
Plentiful ammunition,
Proper clothes,
Sufficient food –
Is it too much to ask?
O my countrymen!
Give us a level playing field,
Give us a fighting chance.

**–Shyam Kumari**

**A Tribute by Pepsi**

*(FICCI had created a "FICCI Shradhanjali – Jawan Trust". A concert had been held and a sponsorship brochure had been released in which the following tribute was given by the PEPSI Company.)*

## A SALUTE TO ALL THE BRAVE SOLDIERS

"We haven't met you yet we know you so well

While we slept, you kept watch

While we bought a new house, you shared a cramped trench

While we stayed warm and dry, you braved sub-zero temperatures

While we listened to music, you endured the sound of gunfire

While we made a new friend, you saw yours die before your eyes

While we received a present, you received a bullet

While we were living up our lives, you were giving up yours

We may not know you but we owe our life to you.

### A Daughter's Tribute

*(My eyes fill with tears when I think of the supreme sacrifice of all the gallant sons of India and the sacrifice of their families too, the anguish the families must have gone through for so many days pre and post war! – Poornima Thapa: youngest daughter of PVC Dhan Singh Thapa)*

### An Ode to the Brave Hearts of Indo China War 1962

This is not dedicated to just one War Hero

This is a dedication to all the War Heroes

The Real Life heroes, sung and unsung

All those soldiers and officers

Who fought valiantly and courageously

Undaunted by the heavy odds.

Nothing deterred them —

Not the harsh, hard terrain

Not the continuous cold winds

Not the dipping minus temperatures
Nothing deterred them —
Not the lack of proper attire
Not the lack of ammunition
Not the lack of preparedness.
Nothing deterred them —
Not the thought of their elderly parents
Not the thought of their young wives
Not the thought of their little children.
Nothing deterred them —
Not the thoughts of the cozy fire in the hearth,
Not the thought of the warm home-cooked food,
Not the thought of their green green pastures
No, nothing deterred them.
Cut off in a cold, harsh terrain
Surrounded by enemies
With superior strength
Of manpower and ammunition
Their only THOUGHT was
"To kill or be killed
To protect OUR MOTHERLAND."
My salutations to their Spirit.
Such souls do not die, ever,
In our heartbeats they live forever.

**–Poornima Thapa**

**Endnote:**

The Indian debacle was more due to the failure of its warped military strategy and lack of military preparedness than due to any failure at tactical level. Throughout the 1950s, the Indian government had paid scant attention to its armed forces. In May 1957, the strength of the Indian Army was 450,000. The government contemplated downsizing it to 150,000 and converting the rest into Labour Corps. General Shrinagesh, then Army Chief, wrote in his diary later, "He (Nehru) agreed that Pakistan was making military alliances, had been contemplating rearming with modern weapons, and had by no means forgotten Kashmir. But when it came to China, it drew a firm 'No' because the Chinese were our trusted friends; and we (army commanders) were foolish, hot headed, and needlessly belligerent. Unfortunately, perhaps, China had not yet built the Aksai Chin Road. We came away with the agreement to a 300,000 force, less than what we had contemplated, but still a force and a military one — not a Labour Corps!"

According to a de-classified Pentagon historical study paper on the Sino-India border dispute, 'Developments between late 1950 and late 1959 were marked by Chinese military superiority, which, combined with cunning and diplomatic deceit, contributed to New Delhi's reluctance to change its policy toward the Beijing regime for nine years'. The study records that 'the Chinese diplomatic effort was a five-year masterpiece of guile, planned and executed in a large part by Zhou En Lai. The Chinese Premier deceived Nehru several times about Chinese maps and carefully concealed Beijing's long-range intentions.' He played on 'Nehru's Asian, anti-imperialist mental attitude, his proclivity to temporise, and his sincere desire for an amicable Sino-Indian relationship' and strung along Nehru by creating an impression through an equivocal language that:

(a) It was a minor border dispute

(b) Beijing would accept the McMahon Line, and

(c) The old Kuomintang period Chinese maps would soon be revised.

The study concludes that "In the context of the immediate situation on the border where Chinese troops had occupied the Aksai Plain in Ladakh, this was not an answer but rather an implicit affirmation that India did not have the military capability to dislodge the Chinese" (Quoted in Chief of Army Staff Gen.V.P. Malik's article in TRIBUNE SPECIAL)

During Dhan Singh's incarceration, the commissars kept harping on the fact that the Indian army had attacked first. Though the Chinese are past masters at prevarication, falsehood and deceit, in this context they had a case. To establish our territorial claims along the McMahon Line, Prime Minister Nehru had embarked on an ill-advised policy fraught with danger — the "forward policy" which entailed the establishment of forward posts and a demarcation and unilateral interpretation of the McMahon line.

But, if this was the eventual goal, why had we deployed an understaffed brigade of only some 3,500 men, when the Indian army had an approximate strength of 3 million? The planning was warped. Indian Intelligence Agencies had no clue. The Army was warning again and again that they were facing 4 or more heavily trained Mountain Divisions. Sadly, our soldiers had World War 1 rifles, while the Chinese had semi-automatic — AK 47 rifles.

The authorities in Delhi never considered that big guns and ammunitions cannot be supplied without an infrastructure, without roads. They did not think of accommodation or of front line fortifications, or about establishing supply routes. There is a famous dictum "An army marches on its stomach". At some places the Government failed to even provide basic tools to dig trenches. Our soldiers were literally using their bare hands to dig trenches. For this lack of foresight our brave soldiers had to pay with their lives.

Moreover according to defense experts the Indian deployment on the north bank of Pangong Lake was unsustainable and, therefore doomed to destruction. Moreover Sirijap 1 and 2 had neither any tactical significance nor any defense potential. The Indian defenses should have been on the high ground to the west within easy turn round distance and maintainable from our base at Phobrang!

# Company Quartermaster Havildar Abdul Hamid

## Birth and Childhood

In district Gazipur of Uttar Pradesh there is a village named Dhamupur. Before 10 September 1965 the name of this village probably never appeared in any newspaper. There was neither a railway nor a paved road leading to the village. Nearly four/five hundred farmers' families lived there. Amongst them was the family of a farmer, Mohammad Usman. On 1 July 1933 Sheikh Usman and his wife Sakina Banu's first son Abdul Hamid was born. Nobody could have guessed that this child would make the name of this village famous in the entire country.

Usman's ancestors had owned lots of land, but with time they lost most of it. When Abdul Hamid was born, the family's worldly possessions had dwindled to some fields, a small tiled house and a sewing machine. The family got some food grains from its fields and Usman earned some money by sewing the villagers' clothes. The family subsisted on these meagre earnings.

### The Son and Grandson of Wrestlers

In the third decade of the 20th Century, India had not gone cricket crazy and the nation's traditional games and highly developed martial arts like wrestling, lathi play and patka and games like kabbadi had neither lost their popularity nor faded into oblivion. Most popular among the indigenous games and martial arts were kabbadi, wrestling and lathi play. In those days almost every village had a wrestling arena.

The villagers of Dhamupur had made a wrestling pit near the village pond. Here, in the evening, after the day's work was done, the villagers practised lathi play and held wrestling matches. Usman was one of the most enthusiastic participants. Due to a lifelong practice of lathi play and wrestling Usman's body had become strong like a rock. In the evenings while on one side of the arena were held wrestling matches, on the other side was practised the art of lathi play. Usman was an expert in both.

Apart from Abdul Hamid's father, his maternal grandfather was also a wrestler. Thus, in a way, Abdul Hamid inherited his expertise in wielding the lathi and wrestling. He took his first steps in the soil of the wrestling arena and maybe he sometimes ate some of that earth. Many an evening, Usman would carry his beloved eldest son and sit him on a piece of cloth on one side of the arena, before starting wrestling and lathi play. The child Abdul Hamid would look with wonder at his father wielding his lathi with lightning rapidity or holding down his opponent in a victorious wrestling hold. Most probably the young Abdul Hamid dreamt of lathi play, kabbadi and wrestling.

### Magician of the Catapult

From an early age Abdul Hamid showed a special aptitude for marksmanship. From his childhood, he began to practice shooting. He had neither a gun nor a pistol, but shot with a home-made catapult, a *gulel.* A catapult is a truly useful thing for a village lad. He can use it in diverse ways. It comes in handy for felling ripe mangoes or guavas, hanging temptingly out of a child's reach from the high branches of trees. Young Abdul and his *gulel* became inseparable, and with it he practiced target shooting for hours.

As his expertise with the *gulel* increased, Abdul Hamid became a passionate hunter. In time he became such a sure shot that he never missed a sitting bird. He began to feel that he had an unfair advantage over these hapless birds, therefore he never targeted sitting birds but such was his marksmanship that even a flying bird could not escape his unerring aim.

**Disinclination for Studies**

Abdul Hamid studied up to class four in his village primary school. Then he studied up to Class 8 in Junior High School, Deva. But he had no interest in studies and he left school after class eight. His parents were naturally disappointed and sometimes reasoned with him and at other times scolded him, as Yashoda scolded and even punished baby Krishna, without realising who he was.

**Unbeaten and Undefeated**

Disinclined to study, Abdul Hamid's interest and genius lay elsewhere. From his childhood he began to learn wrestling and lathi play and by the time he entered his early teens he became a champion in both. None of his opponents could defeat him. In kabbadi even several opponents could not hold him down. Even before entering his teens, he sometimes challenged his own father. Usman would lift him up and throw him to one side of the *Akhada* but secretly he felt proud of his son's strength and daring. Hamid never, ever lost a kabbadi game or a wrestling competition.

**The Swimmer and Boatman of Mangai: the Life Saver**

Near Dhamupur flows the one kilometre wide river Mangai. Villagers bathe and children frolic in its waters. Sometimes fishes dart up and fall back in the water with a splash. During summer the Mangai's flow is placid but in the rainy season it becomes a raging torrent. For Abdul Hamid the river Mangai and its waters were like the lap of his mother Sakina Banu. He swam and played in its waters for hours. Even during the rains, when the river would be in spate and its torrent raged, he would swim the one kilometre stretch of the river with ease. He became such an adept at boating that with the help of his oars he could make a boat dance round and round so rapidly that people on the banks broke out in spontaneous applause.

Once when Abdul Hamid was 14 or 15, a girl fell into the pond near the wrestling arena. He at once jumped in and saved the girl from drowning.

**Escapes to Calcutta**

Abdul Hamid was of a fiery temper and the ordinary world with its simple occupations was not congenial to his temperament. At home there were frequent disagreements and sometimes scuffles between the wayward son and his simple parents who expected their son to follow in the age-old pattern of life that they followed. Once 13 year old Abdul Hamid quarrelled with his parents and ran away to Calcutta. Many people from his village worked in jute mills of Calcutta. He planned to join them. In those days the ticket to Calcutta from his village was only six paisa. Upon alighting from the train he found that the city and the roads were strangely silent and empty. The whole atmosphere was scary. There were dead bodies on the road. All the shops had downed their shutters. It was 1946, the year of the great Calcutta killings when thousands were killed as a prelude to the partition of the country.

Abdul Hamid was bewildered. He was walking on the pavement when the closed shutter door of a shop opened and a hand pulled him inside the shop. He was a kind Hindu shopkeeper. He asked the boy what he was doing in Calcutta. Abdul Hamid told him that he had run away from home and wanted to join some fellow villagers who were working in the jute mills. The shopkeeper told him that Muslims were killing Hindus as they wanted a separate country, Pakistan. Why Pakistan? Abdul Hamid was perplexed because even though his was the only Muslim family in Dhamupur, they had never felt any difference or even discrimination, not to speak of enmity.

The Hindu shopkeeper gave him shelter and food for some days and when the situation became a little normal, he contacted some of the villagers of Dhamupur working in the jute mills, bought a ticket for Abdul Hamid and sent him back to Dhamupur with one of the villagers. His worried parents were relieved to have him back safely.

**Unshakable Resolve to Join the Army**

Since his childhood Abdul Hamid had only one dream, to join the Army. He knew that to join the Army one needed a strong body. As a preparation for his future career he spent most of his time in wrestling, swimming, kabbadi and lathi play. Actually, he was in a mighty hurry to grow up and join the Army.

Sometimes Abdul Hamid would dream that he was a soldier in the Army and fighting the enemy with a 12 bore gun and when he returns after killing the enemy, the whole village welcomes him with drums. Sometimes he dreamt that he was killed by the enemy. But how to join the Army and kill the enemy? He knew that his mother would never allow her beloved son to join the Army.

Meanwhile, Abdul Hamid's life followed the old pattern. He swam in the Mangai, plucked mangoes from orchards, wrestled, wielded his lathi and took part in wrestling contests. He participated with equal enthusiasm in Ramlila and Moharram processions. He was beloved of the whole village. No festival in the village was complete without his participation. Abdul Hamid's family being the only Muslim family in Damupur, the Moharram procession did not take place there. But his fame had spread to nearby villages and he was regularly invited to participate in the Moharram processions there. In Moharram processions usually a group of lathi wielding youths precedes the Tajia. Experts of lathiplay from all the nearby villages participated. Crowds of villagers gathered to watch them exhibit their skills. Before the show started, Abdul Hamid would bow before his teacher Suleiman, who had taught him lathi and banethi (a type of lathi which has two balls at both ends) and would only then step into the arena. He would challenge four or five expert lathi players at the same time. Fighting on all four sides, he would change positions with lightning rapidity and challenge the opponents to strike at his exposed body, glistening with oil. But, try as they did, their lathis never succeeded in touching him. The public was astounded by his bravery. They clapped and raised slogans in his praise. Their combined voices touched the sky. After Abdul Hamid won his Param Vir Chakra, his friend Baccha Singh told Rahi Masum Raza, "Abdul Hamid was a born warrior. Hindustan and Pakistan have come to know of his bravery only now, but we knew it always." (*Chottey Admi Ki Badi Kahani*, Rahi Masum Raza, p. 69.)

## Tailoring

Although a champion in sports, Abdul Hamid disliked tailoring; but after he left school, he had to learn tailoring. His simple mother dreamt of her son earning a lot by stitching the clothes of white officers. Abdul Hamid quarrelled with his mother on this issue. He told her that he would not tailor clothes but instead join the Army. The villagers heard that India was being partitioned and a new country Pakistan was being carved out of India. 14-year-old Abdul Hamid and his friend Bachha Singh wondered why the country was being partitioned. But nobody could answer their questions.

In truth Abdul Hamid was born to wield a rifle, to shoot enemy soldiers, to blow up tanks. To make him take up tailoring was akin to try to yoke a lion to a plough. When resistance was of no use, he reluctantly began to help his father in tailoring. But his aim never wavered; his mind was focused on his heart's desire, to join the Army and to defend the country.

## Early Marriage: Birth of Two Sons

Usman was fed up with his son's aversion to tailoring. Two or three years passed in this tussle of wills. His parents pondered over how to tame their son. Finally they decided to get him married. Aged only 16-17 Abdul Hamid was married to Rasoolan Bibi, a simple girl of his own age. By a strange coincidence, on 1 July 1950, on Abdul

Hamid's 18th birthday, Rasoolan gave birth to their first son Jainul. After two years their second son Ali Hasan was born.

## The Aspiring Soldier

This aspiring soldier was the finest product of India, a true son of the soil. He was nourished by the golden grain of India in an era when the soil was not contaminated by chemical fertilisers and poisonous pest killers, he was nourished by the crystalline waters of Mangai and of the wells of Dhamupur unsullied by burgeoning industrial waste and unmanageable human excreta, he was nourished by an air pure and invigorating unsullied by the fumes of motor vehicles. His body became unalloyed steel by the constant practise of wrestling, kabbadi and lathi play. His aim became unerring by a whole childhood and teen age years passed in hunting birds, by a life lived outdoors, without the burden of a lop-sided mental labour, which is the fate of modern Indian students. Abdul Hamid was a gift of God to India.

### At last Recruited in the Army: 27 December 1954

Though Abdul Hamid loved his wife Rasoolan and sons Jainul and Ali Hasan, his heart was elsewhere. He dreamt of soldiers marching 'left, right, left, right'. He was eager to fight and kill enemy soldiers. Once he along with a friend went to Gazipur, to enroll in the Army. But the two were caught and brought back. Now Abdul Hamid had to shoulder family responsibility. He began tailoring in Gazipur. Meanwhile, in Dhamupur Usman's sewing machine was stolen. The problem of meeting the family expenses became acute. The family had to face extreme poverty. Abdul Hamid returned to Dhamupur with his sewing machine to help his father. But the soft rope of family responsibility cannot chain a lion for long! It had to give way.

One night in December 1954, Abdul Hamid left his parents, his wife and his sons, his friends and his village and ran away to join the Army. This time he went to Banaras and was recruited in the Grenadiers Infantry Regiment with an Army number 2639885 on 27 December 1954. He wrote a letter to inform his parents about his having joined the Army. After getting the news, the whole family heaved a sigh of relief. Usman accepted the inevitable. He knew that his son was like a mountain torrent, which could not be dammed.

### The Recruit Becomes Teacher

After his selection Abdul Hamid was trained at the Regimental Center Nasirabad in Rajasthan. On Abdul Hamid's first day in the Army, the Havildar of his unit lined up his recruits to teach them marching. He was astounded by the expert marching of Abdul Hamid and asked, "Recruit! Have you learnt marching before?" Abdul Hamid answered, "No, Havildar Sahib." "Then how are your steps so controlled?" "I have learnt lathi play Havildar Ji" Abdul Hamid answered. From that day, the Havildar became the student of this new recruit. Abdul Hamid began teaching lathi play to his Havildar as well as to some other recruits.

After completion of his training Abdul Hamid was posted to the 4 Grenadiers Battalion where he would serve for the rest of his service life. His first posting was to Rampur. After serving in the rifle company he was posted to Recoilless platoon in the Support Company.

## The Indo-China War of 1962

Before the advent of this war, India's borders with China were not clearly demarcated. But it was supposed that when people crossed the Hindu Kush, the Karakoram or the Himalayas, they entered Indian Territory. In October 1913 the British had called a conference at Simla where the representatives of both the Chinese and Tibetan governments were present. The Foreign Secretary to the Government of India Sir Henry McMahon proposed that the eastern border between China, Tibet and India should lie along the watershed of the Brahmaputra river; this was accepted by the Tibetan government in 1914. During the Japanese advance into Burma in World War 2 Assam Rifles posts at Walong and Dirang were established on the major routes from Tibet to India. Thus when India became independent, it had boundaries with China which were marked on maps as Macmahon Line but were not demarcated on land. China had not accepted these boundaries. In 1950 China invaded Tibet. India moved forward in Tawang and brought it under its control.

For administrative purposes, India established the North-East Frontier Agency (NEFA) with its headquarters at Tezpur. Meanwhile, China built a road from Sinkiang to Tibet through the Indian territory of Aksai-Chin. Chinese maps showed not only the Aksai-Chin area but also the areas south of the McMahon Line upto the foothills of the Himalayas, as Chinese territory. Since 1956 there had been some tension along the long China-India border and some troops were deployed in this area. Some officers in the Indian Army were apprehensive and brought this to the attention of the Indian Government. But the Government did not take their misgivings seriously. Some of the military officers too, toed the official line.

China was strengthening its grip on Tibet. In March 1959 His Holiness the Dalai Lama escaped to India and the Chinese attacked the Assam Rifles post at Longju. The Government of India entrusted the Army with the operational control of NEFA. 4 Infantry Division, in which Abdul Hamid was serving, was sent from Ambala to NEFA. While the Chinese had been building roads right up to the border, there were hardly any roads on the Indian side and our troops in forward posts had to move on foot carrying their own kit, weapons and other supplies manpack or on mules, or be supplied by air where drops could be made.

After the Chinese attacked the Assam Rifles post at Longju, the Indian Army was ordered to establish 24 new posts along the McMahon Line. Even though the Corps Commander, Lieutenant General Umrao Singh advised against this move, his advice was ignored. One amongst these new posts was Dhaula. The Chinese decided to teach the Indians a lesson. On 9 September 1962 they established their posts opposite Dhaula on Thagla Ridge. Then they proposed talks.

## The War – October to November 1962

Since many years the Chinese had begun their plot to defeat India. They had built roads in Tibet right up to the border and brought their troops and stocks forward. It is said that before starting the war they had dug 30,000 graves in Reema opposite Arunachal Pradesh, to bury the corpses of Indian soldiers. In the beginning, the Chinese began to attack our scattered, unarmed posts in Ladakh and Arunachal. The soldiers manning these posts had neither arms, suitable clothes and shoes nor they had any inkling that war was about to break out. These posts were established just to mark our boundaries. When Nehru was informed that the Chinese had overrun some of our posts, without any knowledge of the ground realities, of how ill-equipped our Army was, or how well-prepared and entrenched were the Chinese, he ordered the Army to throw the Chinese out from our posts. The power-drunk Chinese took this as an insult and a challenge.

Abdul Hamid also participated in the 1962 Operations with the battalion in Khenzemane, Thagla Ridge as part of the 7 Mountain Brigade, under the command of Brigadier John Delvi. 7 Brigade was ordered to move to Dhaula area and Abdul Hamid's battalion was posted at Namka Chou. Lt. General Umrao Singh, GOC 33 Corps reacted strongly against these orders to hustle troops forward without artillery support or administrative back up.

The Indian Government with Krishna Menon as the Defence Minister and General Thapar as the Chief of the Army Staff, decided to ease out Gen. Umrao Singh and replaced him with a more pliable officer, Lt. General BM Kaul, at that time Chief of the General Staff at Army HQ. A new Corps Headquarters, 4 Corps was raised and General Kaul was entrusted with the responsibility of all operations in NEFA.

From 8 October 1962 the Chinese began attacking the Indian posts. The attacks gathered momentum from 15 October. On 19 October, Brigadier JP Delvi, Commander 7 Brigade asked for permission to withdraw from Namka Chou to a position which was more defensible. But still Brigadier Dalvi was denied permission by Gen. Kaul to move to another position. That the Govt. of India and its controversial Defense Minister were ignorant of the intricacies of war, of the thousand hard facts, the instant decisions, the lightning moves needed to face the situation on the battlefield, changing by the minute, is understandable, though not excusable. But the decisions of Gen. Kaul on the spot are neither understandable nor excusable.

What the astute soldier Brigadier JP Dalvi had feared, when he asked to take a defensible position, ultimately happened. On 20 October, at 5 a.m. the Chinese guns and heavy mortar opened up and pounded our positions for one hour attacking our troops from many sides. Our Rajput and Punjabi troops fought with all that they had but what could they do without artillery support! Out of the 513 ranks of Rajputs, 282 were killed, 161 were taken prisoner by the Chinese, and only 60 escaped. By 12:30 p.m. 7 Brigade was scattered and disseminated. The rest of the troops escaped through Bhutan. Brigadier Dalvi and his party lost their way on those fog shrouded peaks and were captured by the Chinese on 22 October.

## The Final Battle: The Escape

Our brave hero Abdul Hamid kept on firing. But one by one the guns of his friends fell silent, while the intensity of the Chinese bombardment increased. Even then he did not lose heart. Soon his ammunition was exhausted. When surrounded by the enemy he, along with some of his fellow soldiers, decided to retreat. Though it is difficult and humiliating for a soldier to abandon his post, it is better to live and fight another day, instead of dying inevitably. Abdul Hamid and two of his friends escaped taking with them their rifles to prevent them from falling into enemy hands.

For 14 days, the three walked stealthily through the snow and sleet-covered unfamiliar mountain paths and ravines, to escape detection by the Chinese. They survived on whatsoever they could lay their hands upon, birds or small rodents they could catch or wild berries and jungle fruits. They sucked ice or drank the ice cold water of mountain streams and on the 15th day reached their base camp, famished and weak. After this operation his unit moved to Ambala and Abdul Hamid was appointed Company Quartermaster Havildar of the Administrative Company.

On 20 November China declared a unilateral ceasefire and on 21/22 November midnight the fighting ceased. China vacated all the posts it had taken and withdrew to the pre-war positions.

### Awarded a Shaurya Chakra: Aims at Winning the Param Vir Chakra

During this battle Abdul Hamid had destroyed a bridge over a stream which had delayed the Chinese advance for a while. He was awarded a Shaurya Chakra for his bravery. From then onwards he dreamt of winning the Param Vir Chakra and told his family about his hope and ambition.

### Home on Leave: Loving Father

By now Abdul Hamid was the happy father of four sons - Jainul Hasan, Ali Hasan, Talat Mahmud and Junaid Alam, and one daughter Najbul Nisar. When Abdul Hamid came home on leave, he taught his sons wrestling. Though a loving father, he was also a strict disciplinarian and if the children did not study or were mischievous, he punished them.

### Shoot by Sound

Many persons shoot unerringly by sight but Abdul Hamid could also shoot by sound. Once, after the 1962 war, Abdul Hamid had come home on leave. One night, while he was talking to his friend Baccha Singh, a bird named *markhaniyan* started chirping. This bird is supposed to be a bad omen by the simple village folks of Dhamupur, who believed that if it chirped, some misfortune was sure to befall them. While the two friends talked, the bird kept chirping loudly. Nobody could sleep. The credulous simple villagers imagined and feared the worst catastrophes.

Abdul Hamid asked his friend Baccha Singh to bring his 12 bore gun and then walked towards the tree from which the sound was coming. It was a dark night. He took aim at the source of the sound and fired a shot and the bird fell down dead. Everyone applauded.

## Pakistan's Perfidy: The 1965 War

After our independence in 1947, it has been seen repeatedly that some invisible Power is guarding our country. It became obvious in 1962 when China, many times more powerful in arms and men than India, could have marched deep into India, nevertheless stopped the war unilaterally and withdrew to the pre-war position. Again, In 1965, when Pakistan suddenly attacked India, at a time when India was not ready psychologically or militarily for war, a war for which Pakistan had been preparing for two years, with a fixed aim to annex Kashmir, while India had no other agenda than to safeguard its borders.

Apart from the advantage which an aggressor generally has in the initial stages of a war, for this 22-days war in 1965, Pakistan had the most modern American armament. Pakistan had received American aid of 1.5 billion dollars. In addition, America had armed Pakistan with 200 M-45 Patton tanks with night vision, which were supposed to be best at the time, and its officers had been trained in America. America also gave to Pakistan one squadron of M-104A supersonic fighter planes, four squadrons of F-86 Saber Jet aeroplanes and two squadrons of B-75 bombers, as well as American side-winder missiles, while India had only subsonic aeroplanes; our first squadron of MIG-21 aeroplanes was being formed and only nine of its aeroplanes were ready for battle. While Pakistan had an atomic submarine like Ghazi, India didn't have even sonar to locate submarines.

General Ayub Khan was Pakistan's President at the time. Since the 1962 defeat at the hands of China, Indian Armed Forces had partially been shaken. The country had also not recovered from the loss in 1964 of their beloved leader Jawaharlal Nehru. Pakistan considered the gentle Prime Minister of India, Shri Lal Bahadur Shastri to be a weak player. They hoped to crush India under him in no time. General Ayub Khan decided that the confidence of Indian Armed Forces being at low ebb, it was the best time to attack and defeat India.

It is a bitter truth that but for the divine Grace and the unlimited courage and valour of our Armed Forces, Pakistan could have defeated India in this war. When Pakistan was threatening to reach Delhi in one day, Bharat Mata filled our soldiers with indomitable courage. At the same time, the Divine covered the eyes of the enemy with pride, which usually comes before the fall. In this war Indian Army taught the Pakistanis a good lesson.

Amongst the many incomparable deeds of valour in the 1965 War, an outstanding one is of India making a graveyard of Pakistani Patton tanks at Khem Karan.

## 'Operation Gibraltar'

From 1963 Pakistan had started preparations for attacking India. It also began a psychological war by inciting the Kashmiris to rebel against India. Pakistan's plan was to push infiltrators into Kashmir to bring about a local uprising and then to send its troops to Kashmir. This plan was code-named 'Operation Gibraltar'.

But before launching Operation Gibraltar the Pakistani Government wanted to probe and test India's response and reaction to an attack on its territory. It also wanted to gauge the reaction of the world powers to its incursion and thirdly, it wanted to test the efficacy of the deadly arms given to them by the Americans.

Therefore the Pakistanis intruded into the Rann of Kutch, an Indian territory of salt covered desert of 23,309 sq. km, of which they claimed 9000 sq. km In January Indian police patrols discovered that Pakistanis had made a track up to two kilometres inside Indian territory. Protests from the Indian side were ignored. India deployed the Central Reserve Police Force (CRPF) on the border to deal with the intruders. On 9 April 1965 a brigade of the Pakistani Army headed by Maj. Gen. Tikka Khan attacked and overran the Sardar and Kanjarcoat posts of India. India sent its 50 Para brigade to check the Pakistanis. Our troops gave Pakistanis a befitting answer.

In June 1965 at the Commonwealth Conference the British Prime Minister intervened and brokered an agreement. India and Pakistan agreed for arbitration and the armies of both countries returned to their positions prior to 1 January 1965. India's restrained response and the mild reaction from the international community reinforced Pakistan's belief that neither the Indian Government, nor the Indian Army had the guts to fight a full fledged, protracted war, and that the Indian reaction to infiltration and war in Kashmir would remain localised and the super powers would not react strongly. Though India had accepted the ceasefire in good faith, a bold decision was taken by the Indian Prime Minister Lal Bahadur Shastri, that any attack on Kashmir would be considered an attack on India and the Indian Army would be free to retaliate when and where it thought fit. He decided, "India can not go on pushing the Pakistanis off its territory. If infiltration continues, we will have to carry the fight to the other side." It was done. The Indian Army decided to capture the bases and routes of the infiltrators. In Kargil Sector the Indian Army captured the posts from where the enemy could threaten the Srinagar-Leh highway. Thus, when the war broke out our Armed Forces were not forced to fight with their hands tied behind their back. They had the freedom to strike at the enemy's most vulnerable points, which they did by capturing the Haji Pir Pass in a bold attack.

Op. Gibraltar had collapsed within one week.

## 1 September: Pakistan Launches 'Operation Grand Slam'

Pakistan failed totally in its objective to capture Kashmir through 'Operation Gibraltar'; rather it was in danger of losing some portions of its occupied territory of Azad Kashmir. To ease the pressure on its troops in Kashmir, on 1 September Pakistan crossed the International Border (IB) and advanced towards Chhamb and Akhnoor.

India had not expected that Pakistan would cross into Punjab. But this time, fully backed by our bold Prime Minister Lal Bahadur Shastri, the Indian Army decided to launch attacks at places of its own choosing across the IB. On 1 September our Chief of Army Staff (COAS) was in Kashmir. He flew back to Delhi and ordered that the plans which had been made in case of Punjab being attacked, were to be put into operation at once. According to the plan, 1 Corps was to launch an offensive from Samba towards Sialkot and X1 corps was to advance towards the eastern bank of Ichogil Canal to Khem Karan, lay bridges across the canal and thus pose a threat to Lahore. By this tactically bold move our Army hoped to bring the Pakistani Army openly into field and be destroyed by our X1 corps. Our Army decided that Asal Uttar would offer a greater chance of victory for our forces than Khem Karan. It was a brilliant plan and the Pakistanis answered on the dotted line. Their armoured units attacked and tried to overrun the 4 Grenadiers' position.

A full Division of Pakistani Armour attacked the Khem Karan area of Punjab. The enemy's aim was to push out Indian forces from Chhamb and take over Jammu and Akhnoor. Had they succeeded India's route to Kashmir would have been cut. At first, Pakistani tanks advanced into India without much resistance. They planned to surround the Indian Army from behind. Flushed by this early victory, Pakistani President Ayub Khan had boasted that Pakistani Army would have lunch in Delhi.

It is said that flustered by the lightning advance of the Pakistani Army some in the Indian Army were in favour of withdrawing our troops to the east of River Beas to dig in and fight there. But Mother Durga chose Lieutenant General Harbaksh Singh as her instrument and filled him with her might. Lt. Gen. Harbaksh Singh convinced the COAS General Chaudhri of the possibility of fighting victoriously on the spot. By his superior strategy of breaching many of the criss-crossing canals of Punjab and a judicious flooding of the roads, Pakistani armour would be bogged down in mud and our Army would make a graveyard of Pakistan's Patton tanks. When Bhakra Dam and its canals were made, nobody had envisaged that one day, in addition to fulfilling their primary purpose of making Punjab the granary of India, their waters would help India to win a war. With the consent of Shri Lal Bahadur Shastri, the Indian army began its march towards Lahore.

A regiment of Pakistani tanks advanced on Bhikkiwind Road and attacked a large area beyond the village Cheema. As mentioned above, due to Gen. Harbaksh Singh's brilliant battle-plan a large area of Punjab was inundated with water. Thus Pakistan's tanks had to come down a narrow road where during a moonlit night, the Indian Army could surround and annihilate them.

Between 8-10 September, the enemy made many efforts to break through the Indian defences. The battle was mainly an armoured battle between the Pakistan 1 Armoured Division with four regiments of Pattons and one Chaffee Regiment and the Indian 2 (Independent) Armoured Brigade with two Sherman and one Centurion Regiment. Though Pakistan was superior in armour, India's skilful flooding of the ground and good tank gunnery thwarted the enemy. In this battle Company Quartermaster Havildar Major Abdul Hamid, 4 Grenadiers won a Param Vir Chakra.

## The Great Warrior Abdul Hamid

Abdul Hamid worked in the military for 11 years. In 1965 the hour of his glory was near. Before the 1965 War broke out, the company commanders and platoon commanders of 4 Grenadiers were sent as an advance detachment to the Indo-Tibet border. Thus when war with Pakistan broke out, the officers of 4 Grenadiers being on Indo-Tibet border, the company officers and seniors from amongst the Junior Commissioned officers were elevated to fight the battle. After 5 years' service in the anti-tank section Abdul Hamid had recently been promoted and given charge of quartermaster stores of his company. As he was the best shot in the battalion, he was reverted to his former charge as NCO commanding the battalion's recoilless rifle platoon. Before the war broke out Abdul Hamid's battalion was given 4 RCLs and Abdul Hamid came to be in charge of this RCL detachment.

In the new defence plan of the Division, 4 Grenadiers, along with three other battalions of the division formed a defence line between Assal Uttar and Chima villages on the Khem Karan-Bhikhiwind-Amritsar road and the Patti axis. 4 Grenadiers was on the northern flank in the general area of Chima village while other battalions were to the south.

## 4 Grenadiers to Fight a Full Armoured Division

Our Army faced a great challenge, such as only the lion-hearted can face, thwart and crush. It was in this battle that the hero of this story would win his Param Vir Chakra. The write up by 4 Grenadiers sums up the situation beautifully: "History is replete with examples of personal bravery in battlefield wherein one man has changed the entire course of the battle with his valour and grit in the face of adversity. CQMH Abdul Hamid belongs to this elite class of warriors. He redefined the meaning of the word bravery in the war against Pakistan in 1965 by almost single handedly defeating the mighty 1 Armoured Division of the Pakistani Army."

There was no time to prepare for an action of this scale. Their Commanding Officer Lt. Colonel Farhat Bhatty deployed 'C' company astride the main axis with 'B' Company in mutual support. Abdul Hamid was entrusted to command the RCL gun of 'C' company.

The Grenadiers had four recoilless guns and some anti-tank mines had been laid in the forward area. But in spite of the shortcomings of Indian defences, the Grenadiers were full of supreme self-confidence. The enthusiasm and joy of battle was coursing through their veins.

4 Infantry Division had been entrusted with the double responsibility; of first, to capture the Pakistani area east of Icchogil canal, the second, to face a possible attack by the enemy on Kasur Khem Karan axis. 4 Grenadiers captured a large area on the Khem Karan-Bhikkiwind road beyond Chima village. The battalion reached the Icchogil canal area on 7 September 1965. But outflanked by the Pakistani counter-offensive, they were ordered back to new positions. They had already been in combat for more than 24 hours when they began digging trenches and weapon pits in defensive positions.

## 8 September: Blowing up the First Tank

Up to the morning of 8 September the trenches were only three feet deep. The battalion-defended area was covered with cotton and sugarcane fields and the battalion was able to camouflage its location, using ploughed fields for field of fire. The 106 mm recoilless guns were deployed along the Khem Karan-Amritsar road. The enemy made many probing attacks. The battalion's recoilless weapons and automatics were effectively sited by the officers of Hamid's company, Lt. HR Jahnu and Lt. VK Vaid. At 7.30 on the morning of 8 September our soldiers heard the rumbling of many tanks. At 9 a.m. they saw a troop of Patton tanks advancing on the road. When the lead tank was 30 yards away Havildar Abdul Hamid of unerring aim, blew it up with his RCL. When they saw the lead tank burning fiercely, the crew of the two following tanks abandoned them and escaped.

Now the enemy began heavy bombardment. It is said that the bombardment was so heavy that a shell fell on each meter of the camping ground of our troops. The second attack came at 11.30 by two troops of enemy tanks covered by heavy artillery fire. Abdul Hamid knocked out the lead tank and again the crew of the following two tanks abandoned their tanks and bolted. Thus Abdul Hamid destroyed two tanks and four Pakistani tanks were abandoned.

In answer to repeated and insistent demands for mines by our troops, soldiers of the Indian Sappers and Miners Company finally laid some anti-tank mines.

## 4 RCL Guns against an Armoured Division

Although the Grenadiers had to face an armoured division with only 4 RCL guns their enthusiasm and morale was sky high because they had already destroyed with their RCLs many more Pakistani tanks than could have been destroyed in an armour against armour, tank against tank battle. It is noteworthy that after firing its first shot an RCL gun can be detected by its big black blast and thus becomes a sitting duck. Therefore it is still more amazing that Abdul Hamid and his crew survived and felled tank after tank for three days.

## 9 September: Saber Jet Attack

On 9 September at 9 o'clock, four Saber Jets attacked the Grenadiers' position but nobody was killed. After the air attack, three armour attacks took place at 9.30, 11.30 and 2.30. The Grenadiers battalion was facing an attack by a whole brigade. By the time the last attack petered out Abdul Hamid's personal tally rose to four tanks destroyed. His battalion had destroyed 13 and many more were blown up in the minefield.

## The Final Shot and Martyrdom

On 10 September at 8:30 a.m. the Pakistanis began heavy bombardment on 4 Grenadiers. On that day, as on the previous two days, the Pakistanis attacked with three tanks. The first tank was advancing in the middle of the road. The other two tanks followed 200 meters behind. Our soldiers had orders to use their ammunition very sparingly. Therefore, it was only when the lead enemy tank reached really close that Abdul Hamid took aim and blew it to smithereens. At 9 o'clock the Pakistanis began heavy bombardment to shield their tanks' advance. Abdul Hamid's gun was mounted on an open jeep. There was real danger of its being blown up by Pakistani bombardment. But Abdul Hamid expertly maneuvered his jeep to shoot the enemy from different positions and angles. Lt. Pantaki helped him in spotting the enemy tanks.

Now Abdul Hamid ordered the other soldiers of his group to take shelter. Thus he was alone in his jeep when another tank advanced from the front. Being alone, Abdul Hamid could not take his jeep elsewhere; therefore, he changed the direction of his gun and took aim. The shell of Abdul Hamid's RCL gun and the shell of the Pakistani tank were fired simultaneously and Abdul Hamid was killed at once. It is not clear whether the last shell that Abdul Hamid fired from his recoilless gun blew up that tank or not, but his battalion believes that this tank was also blown by Abdul Hamid's shell.

## Dream fulfilled: Abdul Hamid Awarded the Param Vir Chakra

Since 1962, when Abdul Hamid had won a Shaurya Chakra in the 1962 War, he had resolved to win the Param Vir Chakra. He sacrificed his life to fulfill his dream. He was given the Param Vir Chakra posthumously and his battalion, the battle honour of Asal Uttar and the theatre honour 'Punjab'.

*RCL Jeep used by Abdul Hamid now at Grenadier Regimental Centre*

## Citation

### Company Quartermaster Havildar Abdul Hamid
### 4 Grenadiers (No. 2639985)

At 0800 hours on 10 September 1965 Pakistani forces launched an attack with a regiment of Patton tanks on a vital area ahead of village Cheema on the Bhikkiwind road in the Khem Karan sector. The attack was preceded by intense artillery shelling. The enemy tanks penetrated the forward position by 0900 hours. Realising the grave situation, Company Quartermaster Havildar Abdul Hamid, who was commander of an RCL gun detachment moved out to a flanking position with his gun mounted on a jeep, under intense enemy shelling and tank fire. Taking an advantageous position, he knocked out the leading enemy tank and then swiftly changing his position, he sent another tank up in flames. By this time the enemy tanks in the area spotted him and brought his jeep under concentrated machine-gun and high explosive fire. Undeterred, Company Quartermaster Havildar Abdul Hamid kept on firing on yet another enemy tank with his recoilless gun. While doing so, he was mortally wounded by an enemy high explosive shell.

Havildar Abdul Hamid's brave action inspired his comrades to put up a gallant fight and to beat back the heavy tank assault by the enemy. His complete disregard for his personal safety during the operation and his sustained acts of bravery in the face of constant enemy fire were a shining example not only to his unit but to the whole division and were in the highest traditions of the Indian Army.

Gazette of India Notification

No. 111 - Press/65

**Footnote:** "Although Abdul Hamid has been honoured with the nation's highest award for courage in the face of enemy, it appears that his citation does not give him full credit for the number of tanks he destroyed. Whereas the Regimental and Battalion Accounts give a detailed account of the seven tanks destroyed by him, it is not clear whether the seventh tank that destroyed him was itself destroyed by him, and as to why the citation gives him credit for only three tanks. After talking to officers who were serving in the unit at that time, and also the Commanding Officer, it transpires that the citation for Abdul Hamid's Param Vir Chakra was sent on the evening of 9 September 1965 after he had knocked out three enemy tanks. On 10 September 1965 he destroyed three more tanks and was killed when he had engaged the seventh enemy tank. When a follow-up message was sent informing the headquarters that Abdul Hamid was no more, the citation was amended to a posthumous award but it appears that the concerned persons failed to amend the total number of tanks destroyed by him to six or seven, as the case may be. The records need to be set right." (*Param Vir Our Heroes In Battle*, Maj. Gen. Ian Cardozo, p. 103.)

## Places of Service

During his service tenure, Abdul Hamid served at Agra, Amritsar, Jammu & Kashmir, Delhi, NEFA and Ramgarh.

## Presentation of PVC Medal

Abdul Hamid's award was announced on 16 September 1965, less than a week after the battle that cost him his life, and was presented to his spouse, Shrimati Rasoolan Bibi by Dr. Sarvepalli Radhakrishnan, then President of India, during the 1966 Republic Day Parade.

### Patton Nagar: Graveyard of Patton Tanks

In the War of 1965 Pakistan had to bear heavy losses. 6,000 Pakistanis were killed in this war, while India lost 2,700 personnel. Pakistan lost 475 tanks while India lost only 80.

Successful action by Indian armour, artillery and infantry anti-tank actions, such as those of Abdul Hamid, tarnished the reputation of the M48 Patton and after the 1965 war, the M48 was largely replaced by the M60. India set up a war memorial named "Patton Nagar" ("Patton Town") in Khem Karan District, where the captured Pakistani Patton tanks are displayed

## Legacy: Mazar at Asal Uttar

10 September is a big day in and around Asal Uttar. The whole area is decorated and people come to pay homage at the Mazar of Param Vir Abdul Hamid. The administration organises a mela, which is very popular among the locals. The residents of Asal Uttar have named a dispensary, library and school after the Param Vir in the village. The Army Postal Service issued a special cover in his honour on 10 September 1979.

In the 1988 television serial "Param Vir Chakra" by director Chetan Ananda, Abdul Hamid's role was played by the famous actor, Naseeruddin Shah.

A pictorial postage stamp of the value of Rs. 3 was issued by Indian Post on 28 January 2000 as part of a series of five postage stamps on gallantry award winners. The stamp had Abdul Hamid's bust along with an illustration of a jeep with a recoilless rifle.

*Mazar of Abdul Hamid*

## Rassolan Bibi Meets Pratibha Patil, the President of India

In 2008, Rasulan Bibi, the widow of the PVC met the President Pratibha Patil with a number of requests, including creation of a military recruitment centre in their village, converting Hamid's home into a memorial, observing the day of his martyrdom at national level and help for his grandchildren to get Government employment.

***Postal Stamp released in his name***

## Memorial in Dhamupur

A memorial to Abdul Hamid was constructed in his village Dhamupur but later fell into neglect. The Memorial was renovated in 2011 by the Flags of Honour Foundation, founded by Rajeev Chandrasekhar, a member of Parliament, on the occasion of the death anniversary of the martyr. A new statue of PVC Abdul Hamid was installed, and the building and garden renovated.

A living embodiment of bravery, Param Vir Abdul Hamid paid his debt to the Motherland by laying down his life. We Indians should take inspiration from his deeds.

**Medals won**

Param Vir Chakra, Shaurya Chakra, Sainya Seva Medal with clasp "Jammu & Kashmir", Samar Seva Medal, Raksha Medal.

*Memorial at Dhamupur village, Uttar Pradesh*

*The bust of Company Quarter Master Havildar Abdul Hamid at the Grenadiers Regimental Centre. Pic. Kind courtesy, 1965-Stories from Second Indo-Pak War by Rachna Bisht Rawat*

*Memorial at Jodhpur made by 4 Grenadiers*

# Lance Naik Albert Ekka

## Birth and Childhood

To Jari, an Adivasi village of District Gumla of Jharkhand State (previously a part of the state of Bihar) goes the honour of being the birth place of PVC Albert Ekka. This village is situated nearly 180 km from Ranchi.

In this remote and interior village of India, on the auspicious date, 27 December 1942, a son was born to Julius and Mariam Ekka. Nobody had an inkling that one day this child would become a great warrior who would bring glory to his family, village and state and would also help India win a war.

The Ekka family are devout Christians. For generations, the family had lived with their few goats and parrots in a small brick house, with unplastered walls and roof beams covered with country tiles. When one enters the house, it seems time has stopped and we have gone back to the 18th or 19th century. A water tap hanging from the outer wall and some plastic chairs kept in the courtyard for guests are the only signs that we are in the 21st century. Like all Adivasi families, the Ekka family lives in closeness and intimacy with nature.

## Primary Education

Julius Ekka enrolled his five year old beloved son in the nearest primary school, *Shishi Patratoli Primary School*, which was situated 6 km from Jari. Thus Albert had to walk 12 km daily to and back from school. But for Albert, instead of being a hardship, it was a daily adventure. On their way to school, Albert and his friends watched the flying birds and flowering trees. They collected wild berries and wild honey. Many types of birds nested on the trees and underneath in the grass lurked small animals.

All around were forests and fast flowing streams with crystal clear waters. Fish were found in abundance in the pristine streams. These forests and streams offered an ideal opportunity to the Adivasi children for bird hunting and fishing. The Adivasis made special arrow heads shaped like toy tops for bird hunting. These arrows only stunned the birds; for hunting animals, they used pointed sharp arrow heads.

These Adivasi children ran with the speed of winds, their hair blowing back. They waded, frolicked and swam in the fast flowing waters. They shot birds with home-made sling-shots and caught fish with home-made bamboo hooks and lines, and sometimes with their bare hands, and thus supplement the frugal meals their mothers cooked. Thus life, for these children of nature, was a constant adventure. Many a time, while engrossed in their daily bird-watching and fishing adventures, the children would suddenly realise that they were getting late for school and then they would run with all their might to school. Sometimes they ran out of the sheer joy of childhood. Thus they became excellent runners and developed strong and hardy bodies.

## Middle School

After Albert passed out of primary school, Julius enrolled him in Nampur Middle School of Bhikampur which is 8 km from Jari. Albert took the extra 4 km walk in stride and now walked 16 km every day. He was an average student but showed lots of interest in games.

## Hockey Captain - Albert Ekka

Albert Ekka was very good at hockey. He had organised a village hockey team. The village boys dug out bamboo roots and out of these roots made hockey sticks and balls. The village hockey team became strong under the captaincy of Albert Ekka. Even now, after seven decades, his childhood friends remember Albert's love for hockey and how due to his expert guidance, their team became strong.

## Recruitment in the Army - Happy Coincidence

After the 1962 China War, the Indian Army started massive recruitment. Julius Ekka's younger brother was in the Indian Army. He encouraged his son to join the Army. On his birthday 27 December 1962, Albert was enrolled through a recruitment rally organised at Bhikhampur. At the age of 20 he had found his true vocation. He was sent to the Bihar Regimental Training Centre Danapur Cantonment near Patna for his basic training.

## Joins the 14 Guards Battalion

In February 1968 Lt. O.P. Kohli of 'B' Company, 32 Guards Battalion was at the Abrera Camp of 32 Guards, (which would be renamed 14 Guards later on) which is 30 km from Kota in Rajasthan. On 13 January 1968, this new battalion was raised and soldiers from different infantry units were joining it. A thin dark man stood before Lt. O.P. Kohli. This young man, from a Bihar Regiment, did not impress Lt. Kohli. But he had passed his Battle Physical Efficiency Test (BPET). Lt. Kohli, later Colonel and winner of a Sena Medal remembers he was, ". . . not much impressed by the unassuming, docile and quiet young man. But the youth was an Adivasi, so I knew he would be physically fit and that was all we needed. Looking at him then, nobody could have guessed what glory Albert was going to bring us." (*The Brave*, Rachna Bisht Rawat, pp 148-149.) To some extent, the credit of nurturing this hero goes to Lt. Kohli also.

The Adivasis live a carefree life, without much thought to appearance. Lt. Kohli remembers that this new recruit Albert never gave any importance to his looks. Whatever size uniform was issued to him, Albert wore it without caring whether it fit him or not. He would never go to the tailor to get his dress altered to fit him. The result was that his clothes hung limply on his thin frame. Lt. Kohli, who was keen on a smart turn out for his unit, upbraided this newcomer for not having his dress altered. He says, "I would often pull his belt which would be hanging at his waist and tell him to smarten up his appearance." (*Ibid.*)

Military life suited Albert. Whenever he came on leave to Jari he held drill classes for the school children of Jari.

## Marriage and Fatherhood

Soon after joining 32 Guards, Albert was married to an Adivasi girl Balamdina, first through a wedding ceremony according to the Adivasi rituals. An Adivasi marriage is a joyous affair, with the whole community dressed in their colourful best, dozens of them with linked hands dancing to the beating of drums. Then the couple were married a second time in a Christian ceremony in the simple church at Jari. Sometime later, a son was born to the couple. He was baptised by the parish priest and was named Vincent. The villagers of Jari always loved and respected Albert, even before he became a national hero.

## Insurgency in Mizo Hills: Ali Ustad

In May 1967, 32 Guards, now renamed 14 Guards, was moved to Mizo Hills where insurgency was at its height. Albert, since his childhood, was an adept in silently stalking a prey and then like a lightning bolt lunge at and attack it. These skills of trekking and shooting acquired during his boyhood proved doubly useful during the Mizo Hills insurgency. Many a time he went hunting and brought his prey to add variety to the simple food served to the soldiers. Also, with the same skill he trekked the Mizo insurgents.

Due to his commendable work, Albert became a section commander even though he was still a lance naik. (Normally a naik is the section commander). A lance naik wears a 'V' shaped stripe on the sleeve of his uniform, as a sign of his rank and a means of recognition. In the Indian Army a lance naik is called "Ustad", a respectful word which means "an instructor". Albert Ekka was given a nick name "Ali", a short form of Albert. Thus the junior Guardsmen called him "Ali Ustad".

Col. Kohli recounted to Rachna Bisht Rawat how during the Mizo operations Albert slowly developed into an innovative and fine fighter, a true warrior: "He was good with his subordinates and his command and control were good, particularly because he was very reserved and did not mix with others or speak much. His face would always remain blank and he would talk only on a need-to-know basis. One could never tell from his face if he was happy or sad, and what he was thinking." (*Ibid.*) In the Mizo anti-insurgency operations, Ali Ustad proved his mettle and gave a glimpse of his coming greatness.

## The Background of Indo-Pak War of 1971

While 14 Guards was fighting a brutal insurgency in Mizo Hills, a fiercer task awaited the Indian Armed Forces. It is necessary to know the background of the War which gave a chance to Ali Ustad to sacrifice his life for his country and win a Param Vir Chakra.

Since the creation of Pakistan, West Pakistanis despised the inhabitants of East Pakistan. They used the resources of East Pakistan to enrich West Pakistan while treating the Bengalis with hardly disguised contempt. This oppression continued unabated from 14 August 1947 to 1971. For the East Bengalis, it was as if the tyranny of British Rule was replaced by an equal or even greater tyranny of their West Pakistani countrymen. As a revolt against this injustice

East Pakistani Bengalis established a new party, the Awami League, under the leadership of Sheikh Mujibur Rehman.

On 7 December 1970 elections were held in Pakistan. The lower house of Pakistan had 313 seats. Since East Pakistan was more populous, this numerical strength gave it an edge on the western wing of Pakistan and thus Awami League acquired a simple majority in the 313-seat lower house of the Parliament of Pakistan.

When Sheikh Mujibur Rehman put out a claim to form a government, West Pakistanis were shocked. To be ruled by the lowly Bengalis, whom they despised as an effeminate race, was something unthinkable for the West Pakistanis who considered themselves a superior martial race, born to rule the Bengalis. On 21 February 1971, President Yahya Khan dissolved his cabinet and imposed martial law in the country. He indefinitely postponed the convening of the National Assembly. The then Prime Minister Zulfikar Ali Bhutto refused to hand over power to Sheikh Mujibur Rehman.

The Bengalis of East Pakistan revolted against this injustice and exploded in fury. Government employees quit their offices and came out on the streets and normal life came to a standstill. Students quit their schools and joined the numerous agitators. The situation was tense. On 3 March 1971, the Pakistani Government imposed curfew in Dhaka. The Pakistani President Yahya Khan recalled Lieutenant General Sahibzada Yakub Khan, who was the Lieutenant Governor and Martial Law Administrator in East Pakistan and appointed in his place Lt. Gen. Tikka Khan. President Yahya Khan told him, "Kill 3 million Bengalis and then the rest of them will lick our hands." To follow the orders of their President, on 25 March 1971, the Pakistani Army started "Operation Blitz". First, they made all the Bengali Army officials lay down their arms and then killed them.

On 25 March 1971 Mujibur Rehman was arrested and on the night of 25 March and in coming days, with unimaginable brutality, the Pakistani Army used machine guns, rocket-launchers, mortars, tanks and cannons for killing the hapless, unarmed civilians of East Pakistan. Their main targets were Hindus, Bengali intellectuals and members of Awami League. In Dhaka in one night alone they murdered 7000 people. Robert Payne in his book *Massacre* writes, "In one week half of the population of Dhaka ran away." It some ways this genocide was as bad as or even worse than Hitler's genocide of the Jews. It is estimated that in April 1971, 30 million people of East Pakistan were uprooted and did not know how to save themselves.

On the orders of their blood-thirsty President Yahya Khan, the Pakistani Army killed nearly 30 lakh East Pakistanis, of whom about 20 lakh were Hindus and 10 lakh Muslims. The Pakistani soldiers killed their own countrymen and even their co-religionists in the most gruesome and sadistic ways. Thousands of women were raped. From Dhaka, the Pakistani troops moved out in the rural areas, burning whole villages and slaughtering the populace indiscriminately.

## Refugee Influx from East Pakistan

From February 1971 onwards, millions of refugees from East Pakistan fled to India to escape the atrocities and genocide by the Pakistani Army. Ultimately, by May 1971, nearly 10 million refugees took shelter in the arms of Mother India. And though a poor country, India housed and fed them all. It is estimated that India spent 700 million dollars on the upkeep of these refugees. Apart from this economic burden, there were grave security problems involved. There was intolerable tension in Tripura and West Bengal. Obviously, India could not carry this burden indefinitely. Our Prime Minister Indira Gandhi pleaded with American President Richard Nixon to check Pakistani President Yahya Khan. But her pleas fell on deaf ears. Nixon, the then President of America, betrayed humanity by turning a blind eye to the genocide in East Pakistan and by ignoring even the repeated pleas of his own envoy Archer Blood posted in East Pakistan.

Prime Minister Indira Gandhi toured Western countries to seek their help to stop Pakistan from its gruesome activities but with no success. With the world leaders telling India that the atrocities and killings in East Pakistan were an internal problem of Pakistan and the refugee problem was India's problem and India should try to solve it bilaterally with Pakistan, in that hour of grave peril,

India stood alone. Indira Gandhi realised that the United States was hostile to India and after Kissinger's hush-hush visit to China, with the resultant break-through in America-China relations, there was a distinct possibility of the United States and China ganging up against India.

## Friendship Treaty with the Soviet Union

To counter-balance this dire possibility, Indira Gandhi accepted an invitation from Alexei Kosygin, the Soviet Premier, to visit Moscow. There she was given a rousing welcome. On 8 August, Andrei Gromyko, the Soviet foreign minister, came to Delhi and on 9 August a "Friendship Treaty" between the Soviet Union and India was signed by Sardar Swaran Singh and Andrei Gromyko. The most critical article in the Treaty was that if either country was attacked, the other would consult "to remove such threat" and "to take appropriate effective measures to ensure peace and security of their countries." This treaty came as a shock to Pakistan. The United States and China were definitely annoyed by it.

But now, India was not totally friendless. By and large, the world does not know about the crucial help the Soviets gave to India in the Bangladesh War.

## War Clouds Gather

The patience of the Indian government was exhausted. There was a public clamour for war. Prime Minister Indira Gandhi realised that India could not feed and house 10 million refugees indefinitely. Therefore war was inevitable. The first decision India had to take was when to attack. During the rainy season the numerous awesome rivers of East Pakistan get flooded and the three main rivers – the Padma, the Yamuna and the Meghna become several kilometres wide, so wide that one cannot see the other shore, and therefore at that time it would not be an easy task for the Indian Army to cross them. Our Chief of Army Staff General Sam Manekshaw (later Field Marshal) had pointed out to Prime Minister Indira Gandhi that if we attacked during the rainy season, the Indian Army would get bogged in the rain-sodden plains of East Pakistan.

Also, because it required time to collect the sizable force necessary for such an invasion, India could not declare war immediately. There was also another reason to delay the attack. During the summer months the mountain passes, from where China could send its troops in support of Pakistan, would be open. The Indian Army needed time to prepare to fight Pakistan on both its western and eastern fronts and in addition to fight China, in case it intervened. There were critical shortages of men and material. Gen. Sam Manekshaw told the Prime Minister that in spite of the public clamour, war would have to be postponed till winter and then victory would be sure.

## The Insurgency in East Pakistan

In East Pakistan, the insurgency against the Pak army raged throughout the summer. Our indomitable Prime Minister Indira Gandhi escalated her backing of the rebels. The Indian Army had direct orders to help and train the rebels. India had to use the Bengalis to launch a comprehensive war of liberation. Five thousand insurgents were trained in the use of elementary field techniques involving ambush, demolition, disruption of lines of communication etc. These guerrillas had the fire of revenge running through their blood. These were men whose sisters and mothers were dishonoured and butchered in front of their eyes.

## Mukti Bahini Training Camps

Amongst the refugees who escaped to India, were men from the East Pakistan police and para military personnel who had deserted their posts, volunteer youth, NCC cadets, police personnel etc. Their military leaders were mostly inspector and sub-inspector rank officers of East Pakistan Rifles. Apart from them, amongst the refugees, there were lakhs of other youths, most of them in early twenties but some as young as ten years, who were eager to punish the Pakistanis for their inhuman atrocities. They were afire with a desire to liberate their country from the tyrannical rule of Pakistan and establish an independent nation 'Bangladesh'.

Training camps for Mukti Bahini volunteers were set up under Indian Army officers. Thousands of these East Bengali guerrilla fighters, scantily clad, some of them did not have even shoes, ill-armed, hastily trained, would sacrifice their lives in the coming days to establish their dream country 'Bangladesh'.

## 14 Guards chosen to lead the Assault on the Eastern Front: Battles Before the War

Let us move to the Eastern Front, where the hero of this story Albert Ekka was going to win a Param Vir Chakra. When Pakistan launched an attack on 3 December 1971 on the Western Front, India was fully prepared to literally cut Pakistan to size. Indian Army took the offensive in the Eastern Sector, where it was to achieve a glorious victory, in which 94,000 fully armed Pakistani soldiers would abjectly surrender before the Indian Army. Pakistan would be truncated and a new nation 'Bangladesh' would be born.

14 Guards Battalion, a part of 57 Mountain Division, would play an important part in this victory. Its GOC Maj. Gen. B Gonsalves planned that 73 Mountain Brigade under Brigadier Tuli was to capture Ganga Sagar. Capture of Ganga Sagar, especially its railway station, would almost certainly ensure cutting off the enemy supply lines and delay re-enforcements from reaching their frontlines.

## Lt. Col. Vijay Narain Channa: Fire Brand New CO of 14 Guards

The senior officers of the Indian Army were impressed by 14 Guards performance in Mizo Hills. Its officers were already training Mukti Bahini fighters. Therefore, they chose 14 Guards to lead the assault on Ganga Sagar. It was a great honour for this young battalion. 14 Guards was to concentrate at a place called Dukli, which is approximately 6 km from Agartala. Before moving to Dukli, Lt. Col. Vijay Narain Channa took over the command of 14 Guards and the credit of the success of 14 Guards in the battles of Dhalai, Ganga Sagar, Tungi and of leading the Indian Forces to secure Dhaka airport goes to him.

## Battle of Dhalai

14 Guards moved quickly to Agartala on the Tripura-East Pakistan border and were in position by 1 November 1971. North-east of Agartala was located a small town called Kamalpur. Three kilometres across the border opposite Kamalpur were located three Pakistani companies in the Dhalai tea gardens' area. From there the Pakistani soldiers often raided Indian territory. The Brigade Commander called a conference and gave the task to 14 Guards to destroy the Pakistanis in Dhalai. After a fierce battle the Pakistani intruders were chased away. 84 Pakistanis were killed and a huge amount of arms and equipment were recovered. This success of their battalion raised the spirit of our troops sky high.

## A 'Barakhana' and a Fiery Speech

From time to time, our soldiers are served feasts with additional delicacies like *puris, khir, raita* and sometimes rum also. These feasts are called 'Barakhana'. To celebrate the victory at Dhalai and to further motivate his soldiers for the coming battle of Ganga Sagar, Lt. Col. Channa arranged a Barakhana in that jungle concentration area Dukli for his brave soldiers. Petromax lamps were lit and soldiers sang jolly songs. Congratulating his soldiers for their bravery at Dhalai, Lt. Col. Channa gave a fiery speech which set the hearts of his soldiers aflame. Courage and love for the country, coupled with the noble ideal of self-sacrifice coursed through their blood. Such were the words that each of them, even after 47 years, was etched deep in the memory of the then Lance Naik Devendra Nath Das, though Lt. Col. Channa himself has now forgotten them.

Like a lion he roared, "My boys, you will create history for our Nation. I assure you I will bring everybody alive from the war but if we lose some, our history will be written with their blood and their sacrifice. I am very proud of you. . . ."

## On the Path of Glory: The Battle of Ganga Sagar

14 Guards was soon to win a Battle Honour, a Theatre Honour, a Param Vir Chakra, a Vir Chakra and a number of other gallantry awards in the forthcoming battle of Ganga Sagar.

An initial plan to conventionally assault the enemy with armoured support was discarded, as any direct confrontation would have inevitably resulted in heavy losses. Eventually, a reconnaissance/patrol party was formed. The objective of this group was to review the situation from deserted village, Maniad, which was close to Ganga Sagar, and identify gaps or weaknesses in the enemy defences.

The Ganga Sagar Complex was comprised of Ganga Sagar Railway Station, Goal Gangail, Lilahat, Triangle and Mogra. The main Pakistani defences in the Complex were based on the high ground around the railway station. The enemy had utilised the nine month period before the war started to strengthen its positions. The built up area of Ganga Sagar was fortified with sand bags. The marshes which surrounded the area formed a natural obstacle. The few gaps were heavily mined. The main positions were wired and *panjis* (sharpened bamboo sticks) were stuck in the ground. Soldiers would have got impaled if they fell on these lethal *panjis*.

The CO directed all company commanders to carry out a recce (reconnaissance) of Ganga Sagar for effective planning. CO and company commanders went on recce a couple of times. It soon became clear to the recce group that the enemy was well dug in, had strengthened its defensive perimeter by extensively mining the area around the township. The enemy had made a number of underground bunkers along the railway line. There was a big pond and shell proof bunkers were made on all sides.

The recce team saw a handful of Pakistani troops pushing a rail-wagon over the tracks. This indicated that the area between the tracks was not mined and could be used to attack and breach the enemy defences. Back at the base, the CO and his team of officers pondered over the idea of attacking the enemy in a single file. In spite of the underlying risks the officers were confident of the feasibility of their plan to achieve success with minimal loss of life and equipment.

Due to the enthusiasm, determination and the confidence shown by 14 Guards, the higher command gave their consent for the battalion to go into full battle readiness and execute their plans to capture the objective

## Battle Preparation: The Attack Begins

The battalion made sketches of Ganga Sagar. The CO gave a thorough briefing and explained everything in detail, clarified every doubt so that everyone in the battalion was aware of his task.

On 1 December 1971 at about 4 p.m. the battalion left the unit location and moved forward. They crossed the International Border at midnight. The companies infiltrated to Maniad during the night hours. The move through the marshy patches, full of leeches, was slow and exhausting. At one place the men had to cross a 200 meter long pond through metre deep water. The mules had to be unloaded here and the mortars had to be carried by the men and one 106 mm recoilless gun was dismantled and carried on two modified bicycles. This innovative spirit of Indian Army was much in evidence in this short war.

On 2 December 1971, early in the morning, they reached a place called Majhigacha. On 3 December, at 2 a.m., 'A' and 'B' Companies left the concentration area for the attack on the railway station.

## Nothing Succeeds Like Success

Our troops had to attack in total silence to take the enemy by surprise. It was dark and foggy with visibility down to less than 10 meters. 'A' Company led by Maj. Tara and 'B' Company steered by Maj. O.P. Kohli approached enemy lines from each side of the rail-track. This track was laid on an embankment 8-10 feet high and of about the same width. Because the width was so narrow, the troops had to move in single file on either side of the track.

## Dare Devil Albert Ekka Eliminates a Light Machine-Gun (LMG)

When the troops were approximately 40 meters from the nearest Pakistani bunker, a trip wire was disturbed by one of the guides and illuminated the general area of leading troops. With this illumination, Albert Ekka was exposed and challenged by a Pakistani soldier standing in the open on the side of a LMG bunker "Kaun Hai Wahan ?" (Who is there ?) Our hero Albert Ekka roared, "Tera Bap" (your father). At this all hell broke loose. The Pakistanis fired flare after flare. There was continuous rattle of LMGs and MMGs raining bullets. Bravo Company had moved close to the enemy lines next to the pond. They came under heavy fire. It was a grim battle scenario. Pakistanis directed their LMG and MMG fire at our troops. The hellish din of exploding shells drowned the battle cries of our brave jawans. Albert Ekka moved swiftly to eliminate the LMG threat. He lobbed a grenade inside the LMG bunker and then jumping inside bayoneted the soldiers in the machine-gun trench. During the action he was shot in the stomach.

## Maj. A.K. Tara Pulls Out a Medium Machine-Gun (MMG)

Meanwhile deadly fire was aimed at the soldiers of 'A' Company, from a MMG bunker built on the right side of the railway track. The situation at that time was critical. Realising that the MMG bunker had to be neutralised fast, Maj. Tara threw a Molotov cocktail in the bunker, followed immediately with a hand grenade, temporarily stunning the enemy. Before the enemy could recover, he caught hold of the blistering barrel of the machine gun and pulled it out of the dugout and shot dead the two remaining enemy soldiers who were still inside the bunker.

## Glorious Martyrdom of Albert Ekka

The one mile distance from that bunker where our hero Albet Ekka had destroyed an LMG, to the Ganga Sagar railway station was a death trap for our troops. There were underground and overground concrete bunkers, well protected by sand bags and surrounded by sharp panjis and guarded by fully armed Pakistani troops. Albert Ekka was one of the group leading the assault. These brave sons of India in the front line, destroyed these bunkers one by one. Albert Ekka risked his life again and again.

At last, after a long grim fight, the advance party of the battalion reached the Northern Railway two storey signal building. From a bunker made on the first floor of this building a MMG was continuously firing on our soldiers, inflicting heavy casualities. If our troops were to advance the MMG had to be silenced.

Although wounded, Albert Ekka, now set his eyes on taking down this MMG, stationed on higher ground. Under heavy enemy fire, he cautiously crawled towards the bunker and was hit again in the neck. The impact of the bullet made him fall. Regardless of his bullet wounds, unmindful of the pain and the blood loss, he kept crawling forward and managed to reach under the bunker. Squirrel like he climbed a side wall and edged-up close enough to the opening of the bunker. Then he took a grenade attached to his belt and after removing the pin with his teeth, he lobbed it inside through a gap. The exploding grenade shredded into pieces one of the soldiers manning the MMG. But the other soldier was still bent over the MMG. Then our hero Albert Ekka exhibiting supreme will power and complete disregard to personal safety, entered the top bunker, took his rifle from his shoulder and attacked the soldier with his bayonet again and again till he collapsed.

The deadly MMG fell silent, but alas, while climbing out of the bunker Albert Ekka was fatally wounded. He was given first aid but to no avail. The hero succumbed to his injuries. A true soldier, he died in his blood-soaked uniform, with his boots on. This sacrifice of Albert Ekka limited the potential of high casualties and gave a chance to our troops to move forward.

The extraordinary bravery of Albert Ekka had turned the tide of the battle. Free of the deadly bullets of that MMG, our soldiers surged forward and won the battle of Ganga Sagar. By his initiative, courage and self-sacrifice Albert Ekka, who took the bullets of the defenders of the bunker on his chest, had played an important part in securing this victory. He gladly sacrificed his life for the country. Surely angels from heaven must have come to escort the soul of Param Vir Albert to heaven.

## The Param Vir Chakra

On 13 January 1972 Lance Naik Albert Ekka was posthumously awarded the only Param Vir Chakra awarded in the 1971 War in the Eastern Theatre. On 26 January 1972, Mrs. Balamdina, the widow of Lance Naik Albert Ekka received the Param Vir Chakra from the hands of the President of India.

## Citation

### Lance Naik Albert Ekka

### 14 Guards (No. 4239746)

Lance Naik Albert Ekka was in the left forward company of a battalion of the Brigade of Guards during their attack on the enemy defences at Ganga Sagar on the Eastern front. This was a well-fortified position held in strength by the enemy. The assaulting troops were subjected to intense shelling and heavy small-arms fire, but they charged onto the objective and were locked in bitter hand-to-hand combat. Lance Naik Albert Ekka noticed enemy light machine-gun (LMG) inflicting heavy casualties on his company. With complete disregard for his personal safety, he charged the enemy bunker, bayoneted the two enemy soldiers and silenced the LMG. Though seriously wounded in the encounter, he continued to fight alongside his comrades through the mile deep objective, clearing bunker after bunker with undaunted courage. Towards the northern end of the objective one enemy medium machine-gun (MMG) opened up from the second storey of a well-fortified building inflicting heavy casualties and holding up the attack. Once again this gallant soldier, without a thought for his personal safety, despite his serious injury and the heavy volume of enemy fire, crawled forward till he reached the building and lobbed a grenade into the bunker killing one enemy soldier and injuring the other. The MMG however continued to fire. With outstanding courage and determination Lance Nail Albert Ekka scaled a side wall and entering the bunker, bayoneted the enemy soldier who was still firing and thus silenced the machine-gun, saving further casualties to his company and ensuring the success of the attack. In this process however, he received serious injuries and succumbed to them after the capture of the objective.

In this action Lance Naik Ekka displayed the most conspicuous valour and determination and made the supreme sacrifice in the best traditions of the Army.

Gazette of India Notification

No. 7 – Press/72

***Stamp released by Army Postal Service 3 Dec 1978***

## Victory: Ceremonial March into Dhaka

After the victory of Ganga Sagar, crossing the mighty Meghna in local boats on 14th December morning, 14 Guards reached Tungi and in a fierce engagement killed a number of enemy troops. There, they received the news of Pakistani Army's surrender and a message that 14 Guards Battalion was to lead the ceremonial victory march into Dhaka. To lead the ceremonial victory march, after a swift and grim battle was the crowning glory for 14 Guards, this young, probably the youngest, battalion of the Indian Army. At 3 p.m., the proud soldiers of 14 Guards commenced their victorious march into Dhaka. Surely, the souls of Albert Ekka and other martyrs of the Indian Army would have rejoiced in heaven.

## The Last Rites of Albert Ekka

The martyrs' souls climb to heaven but their mortal remains are left behind, for us to cherish, guard and perform their last rites. 14 Guards took their dead to their concentration area Dukli. The last rites for all the martyred soldiers of 14 Guards were performed according to their religion. Albert Ekka's sacred body was buried with the bodies of other Christian martyrs. After the War, before leaving for Mizo Hills, on their post war posting, 14 Guards constructed a War Memorial at Dukli.

## Albert Ekka Memorial and a Shahid Mela in Jari

An Albert Ekka memorial has been built in the village of Jari. One full size statue of PVC Albert Ekka has been erected there. Each year on 3 December, to commemorate the martyrdom of Albert Ekka, Retd. Sergeant Anirudha Singh organises a Shahid Mela (Martyr's Fair) at Jari. Ranchi Army Division Headquarters personnel, along with Army Medical Camp, Welfare Team and CSD Canteen also visit Jari on the occasion of this fair.

*Memorial at Jari Village*

## The Sacred Soil

In November 2015, Mrs Balamdina Ekka met the Chief Minister Raghubar Das of Jharkhand and requested to bring home the relics of her husband. She pleaded, "If it is not possible to bring his relics, kindly get some soil from his grave. Then I can die in peace." Her anguished plea moved the CM. He conveyed the request to Retd. Sergeant Anirudha Singh, organiser of the Shahid Mela at Jari. Anirudha Singh and Maj. D.N. Das at once contacted Lt. Gen. Manvendra Singh (previously of 14 Guards), who was then the Commandant Indian Military Academy Dehradun and requested his help in getting the grave soil from Dukli. They informed Lt. Gen. Manvendra Singh that there was a War Memorial in Dukli, which had been constructed at the cremation/burial site of the martyrs of 14 Guards. By God's Grace, the younger brother of Lt. Gen. Manvendra Singh, Mr. Yadevendra Singh was at that time the DIG of Border Security Force at Agartala. Lt. Gen. Manvendra Singh requested him to get the sacred soil of the grave of Albert Ekka collected from Dukli.

*Statue at Albert Ekka Chowk, Ranchi*

## The Grand Homage: Flowers-Flowers All the Way

On 28 November 2015 a B.S.F. patrol collected the sacred soil from Dukli and sent it to Kolkata through a special courier. There was a big reception party, including many ministers and journalists, to receive the sacred soil. It was brought to CM's office in Ranchi. The CO of 14 Guards sent one Subedar and one Havildar in ceremonial uniforms to escort the Urn containing the soil to Ranchi.

The soil was put in a decorated vessel, which was placed in a flower laden open vehicle. Subedar Ram Chander of 14 Guards in ceremonial uniform escorted the vehicle carrying the vessel. The vehicle was brought to the city centre of Ranchi, which had been named Albert Ekka Chauk in honour of our hero. All the high officials and ministers and other dignitaries welcomed and paid homage to the sacred soil.

*The holy soil is greeted by School Children*

From there began the unforgettable 200 km journey of the Soil-Urn to Jari. Motorcycle riding Police Commandoes escorted the procession. 100 cars, jeeps and scooters followed the flower draped open vehicle carrying the Urn. Throughout the 200 km journey, students and the general public stopped the convoy to pay homage.

They threw flowers and offered garlands at the Urn. The enthusiasm of the public was so great that the convoy could move only at a slow pace.

At Jari the Urn was kept on a stage erected for the function. Five state ministers of Jharkhand were present. The Chief Minister Raghubar Das came in a helicopter and went to PVC Albert Ekka's house to bring Mrs. Balamdina to the venue of the function. Then the Urn containing the soil was ceremonially handed over to her. A plaque was erected at the designated place. On the CM's request Maj. D.N. Singh narrated the story of the battle of Ganga Sagar.

The Jharkhand Government has named a block after PVC Albert Ekka. It was the first block to be named after a Param Vir Chakra recipient. PVC Albert Ekka's only son Vincent works in this block. He gets nearly 30 thousand rupees per month. Mrs Balamdina also gets monthly pension of Rs. 25,000. Sometime back Baba Ramdev went to felicitate the widow of the Param Vir and offered her Rs. one lakh. The Government had given the family a house in Patna and a shop in Ranchi. But the simple Adivasi Ekka family seems incapable of managing finance. Other people took possession of the shop and the house. They live in an old two roomed house with unplastered walls and roof of country tiles, with their parrots and goats. There is a two roomed cement house also, which is equally dilapidated. A proper house should be made for the family.

## An Ardent Desire of Martyr's Widow Mrs. Balamdina

Mrs Balamdina has expressed a desire that a Sainik School should be established in Jari village. Then the children of their village would follow in the footsteps of her husband. Though Jari is developing, many dreams of the inhabitants of that area have not yet been realised. She says, "Many of the villages are situated deep in the interior and the children of those villages cannot go to city schools to study, due to lack of money. Whatever little they earn is spent on food and clothes etc. If a Sainik School is opened in Jari, then they can easily study here."

Faradin, the younger brother of PVC Albert Ekka, who had also served in 14 Guards from 1973 to 1994, says, "If Army recruitment camps are held here in Jari, then many of the Adivasi youth will enter the Army and become patriots."

*Mrs Albert Ekka showing PVC to Maj Das*

*Vincent Ekka - Albert Ekka's only son in front of their house*

## Endnote: A Great Compliment

American journalists are generally critical of India but, in this war, they too were all praise for Indian Army. Maj. Gen. DK Palit in his book *The Lightening Campaign* recalls the comments of Sydney Schanberg of the *New York Times*, who accompanied the Indian troops in two sectors . . ., "I don't like sitting around praising armies. I don't like armies because armies mean war – and I don't like wars. But this (the Indian) army was something. . . . They were great all the way. There was never a black mark. . . . I lived with the officers and I walked, rode with the jawans – and they were all great. Sure some of them were scared at first – they wouldn't be human if they weren't. But I never saw a man flinch because he was scared. There is a tremendous spirit (in the Indian Army) and it did one good to experience it. . . . I have seen our boys in Vietnam – and this army was different. Their (the Indian Army's) arms and equipment aren't as good – but what they had, they used with effect. . . . and could they improvise! I saw recoilless guns carried on shoulders, big guns pushed across marshes like ox-carts, by jawans, villagers, officers, and everybody was in it together. . . . And they were the most perfect gentlemen – I have never seen them do a wrong thing – not even when they saw just how bestial the enemy had been." (*Ibid.*, p.157.)

# Rifleman Sanjay Kumar

## Birth And Childhood: In the Land of Brave Hearts

Himachal Pradesh is called "The Land of Gods". It may also be called "The Land of Brave Hearts".

In Bilaspur district of Himachal Pradesh nestles a village called Baccain. Baburam, a resident of this village, joined the Indian Army as a soldier and was posted to 09 Jammu-Kashmir Rifles. Fighting bravely, he was martyred in the 1965 war with Pakistan. It seemed his young widow Bhagdai faced a dark future.

### Widow of a Martyr: Mother of a Param Vir

But Bhagdai was not destined to lead the bleak life of a hapless Hindu widow. As chance would have it, Baburam's elder brother Durgaram Thakur had become a widower. He married his martyred brother's widow.

Shri Durgaram Thakur and Bhagdai gave birth to three sons and three daughters. On 3 March 1976 their youngest son was born. The couple named the child "Sanjay Kumar". The humble parents never imagined that one day this child would win the highest bravery award of the country, that one day he would become one of the 21 brightest stars in the firmament of the Indian Army.

## A Martyr's Temple

In Sanjay's house his martyred uncle Baburam's photograph was placed in a separate room, where his military dress, cap, medals and other sacred memorabilia were cared for with reverence. Few children are so lucky as to have a temple of one's hero, one's ideal in their own home. The story of their uncle Baburam's bravery and the memory of his martyrdom coloured the emotions of all the three sons of Durgaram and Bhagdai, especially so of the youngest, Sanjay Kumar. The three youngsters decided to join the Army and to live or if so required to die for the motherland. The parents supported their sons in their aspiration.

Day and night our hero Sanjay Kumar had only one dream, one aim; to follow in his martyred uncle's footsteps and join the Army. Ordinary children quake at the very idea of death but Sanjay and his brothers had conquered the fear of death right from their childhood. To them no aim was nobler than to die in the service of the country.

Sanjay was educated at the high school of Kalol where he became an N.C.C. cadet and participated in several N.C.C. camps. He loved shooting. There was a 12-bore Indian rifle in their village and whenever Sanjay's brothers went hunting, they took Sanjay along. While boys of Sanjay's age played marbles, cricket or Kabbadi or simply loitered around, Sanjay made an acquaintance with firearms and attained some proficiency in shooting. In a way, this practice for rifle-shooting was an early preparation for his military career.

In 1993 Sanjay passed his matriculation examination. He requested his father to enrol him for further education. But sadly Durgaram had no money to further educate his son. Apart from paucity of funds, Durgaram, a simple soul, was afraid that living in a strange city, far from home, without parental supervision his son might go astray. Therefore after matriculation Sanjay's education was discontinued and he came to Delhi in search of a job.

## A dream comes true

Sanjay recounted, "From 1993 to 1995 I took up a job in Delhi. I was fond of driving; therefore, I learnt to drive jeeps and cars. My cousin's husband was an inspector in the Tibet Border Police. He used to suggest, 'Sanjay, why don't you join the police? After all the difference between the army and the police is only the colours of the uniform - green or khaki!' But I was resolute; 'Come what may, I will join only the Army.' After two years' service in Delhi, I returned to Bilaspur and became a taxi-driver. But my ardent desire and resolve to serve in the Army was unshakable and whenever there was any recruitment for the Army, some of us friends applied together. Two of my friends were selected for the Army. In 1996 the rest of us applied to the Jabalpur Centre for recruitment. Per application we could appear for examination three times. I went to the January recruitment examination but did not succeed. I went again in March and was again unsuccessful. But I did not lose hope because I had faith that some time or other my hard work and my family's prayers would bear result. When I went to the May recruitment I was selected. I was 21 years old at that time. It was my last chance. In June the orders for my selection and training arrived. Thus mine and my family's dream was fulfilled.

## Appointment in 13 Jammu and Kashmir Rifles: Battle with Terrorists

"I ardently desired to join my uncle's Regiment - the 09 Jammu-Kashmir - in order to serve the country, and God fulfilled my aspiration. Though not to his unit, I was posted to his battalion.

"On 26 June 1996, I was sent to Jabalpur for training. On 28 April 1997, after one year's training, I was appointed to the battalion of my dreams, 13 Jammu-Kashmir Rifles and was sent to Bairakpore, Kolkata. After only three months' stay in Kolkata, in July 1997 our unit was sent to Srinagar-Sopore, where the battle lines are drawn between the terrorists and the Army. During 1997-1998 we worked in that terrorist-infested area. In those two years my unit killed many terrorists but we also lost several of our comrades. War is cruel indeed!

## The War Begins

"After battling the terrorists for nearly two years, in April 1999 I came home on one month's leave. During that period I got engaged to a girl named Pramila. When my leave was over, I returned to my unit and came to know that Pakistani soldiers had sneaked into our territory and had occupied several areas of our sacred motherland and that our unit was being sent to Drass to throw them out. Our hearts were filled with enthusiasm and joy for the coming battle. We were overjoyed because we had been in the Army for only 2/3 years and yet were to get the honour of fighting for our country. We were being given a chance to show our bravery, to honour our pledges and to defend our country. A soldier seeks to join the Army with this single aim. The time had come to fulfill our pledges and our vows. We were proud that while there are many soldiers who never get to fight, we were among those who were getting a chance to fight for our country and in the process were sure to win accolades for our unit and regiment. Eager for battle, ready to kill or get killed, sure of victory, we marched towards Drass."

## The Intelligence-Failure of India

At the beginning of the Kargil War India had supposed that the intruders in Kargil were illiterate or half-educated, radical mujahiddin. In fact the infiltration was carried out by the *Northern Light Infantry* of Pakistan, who, in February 1999, launched 'Operation Badr'. Four to seven battalions of *Northern Light Infantry* led by their officers, silently waded in waist deep snow to climb to the snow-clad Kargil peaks. Selected members and commandos of *Special Services Group* of Pakistan accompanied them. Mujahiddin carried the Pakistani Army's luggage. Upon reaching the peaks, the Pakistanis pitched their special North Pole tents, suitable for living in the snow. They thus controlled approximately 130 to 200 square km of dominating heights along NH 1D. After the Kargil war was over, the Indian Army found the Pakistani Army's registers which made it clear that the Pakistanis had been on Indian soil since February 1999. The Pakistanis had made bunkers and *sangars.* (After digging trenches on peaks, small walled hiding places are built from the stones dislodged while digging. These are called *sangars. Sangars* do not have strong roofs like bunkers. They can be destroyed by hand grenades. But for throwing hand grenades at *sangars* soldiers have to come quite close. They have to hold on to the mountain-side with one hand and throw the hand grenade with the other. These hand grenades are quite heavy and soldiers have to come up to within 15 to 17 meters of their object, which is dangerous. Nowadays, our commando companies are supplied with automatic grenade launchers.)

The fully-trained and well-equipped soldiers and officers of the *Northern Light Infantry* of Pakistan penetrated up to several kilometers inside India, built new bunkers, and after climbing the mountain tops of Tololing, Tiger Hill, Bajrang and Batalik, occupied the bunkers built by the Indian Army. Due to the inexcusable negligence of our Intelligence Agencies this large-scale incursion by the enemy was not detected. Even the pictures taken by our satellites and helicopters failed to record the enemy presence. The 121 brigade of the Indian Army was posted in that area but it was as if they had shut their eyes and plugged their ears and thus remained unaware of the enemy movement. In fact our Army had erroneously assumed that there would be no more wars with Pakistan. This wishful thinking and self-delusion had lulled them into a false sense of security. Their vigilance became perfunctory.

The Pakistanis hoodwinked us. They entrenched themselves so well and placed their guns so strategically that when in May-June 1999 the snow-bound Zojila pass opened for traffic, they made it impossible for any vehicle to travel on the Srinagar-Leh highway. Their scheme was to place their guns on the mountain tops of Kargil and thus have every vehicle on the Srinagar-Leh highway in their sights — a sitting duck for them to shoot and to kill the soldiers being transported on that route and thus sever the connection of

Ladakh with Kashmir, and also cut the supply line to Siachen and starve to death our soldiers posted at Siachen.

In February 1999 the bombardment by the Pakistanis blew up two of our Arms Depots. Though our military authorities were concerned at the enhanced activities of the Pakistani Army, they could not gauge the seriousness of the situation and continued in their belief that this was a camouflage for pushing in extra mujahiddin and terrorists into India. To hoodwink India and the world the Pakistani Government made loud noises about the so-called mujahiddin who were soon going to liberate Kashmir. Thus they successfully duped our Army.

**The saviour of Kargil in 1947-1948 - Major General K.S. Thimmaya**

In the context of the 1999 Kargil War it will be in the fitness of things to remember how another great hero, Major General K.S. Thimmaya, who, during the 1947-1948 War, saved Kargil for India, by an undreamt of and unheard of feat of taking tanks to the 12,000 feet high Zojila Pass. Our first war with Pakistan was fought just a few months after the Partition of the country, when the soldiers of Pakistan's *Gilgit Scouts,* aided by tribals and other Pakistani Army regulars attacked Kashmir.

But for heroes like Major General Thimmaya who was commanding the Srinagar Division in 1947-48, we would have lost Kargil, as we have lost the area called Pak Occupied Kashmir. During the Burma War Major General Thimmaya had seen tanks climb up hills. In September Lt. General K.M. Carriappa (later Field Marshal) asked his officer Lt. Colonel (later Major General) Rajinder Singh Sparrow: "Can you break through Zojila with your tanks?" This work had to be done within one month, by the end of October, and that too in utmost secrecy. He answered, "Yes."

Maj. Gen. Lehel said, "Absolute surprise was very important. If the enemy found out and placed two anti-tank guns on the pass, we would have failed. Also, there was a problem with bridges. The tanks were moving from Jammu and the wooden bridges wouldn't be able to take their load. To overcome the problem the turrets of the tanks were removed to lighten the weight. The ammunition was carried separately." (*Despatches From Kargil*, Srinjoy Chowdhury p. 27.) To hoodwink the enemy during the 300 kilometers long journey from Baltal to Zojila our Army dressed the tanks to look like T-16 infantry track carriers. Maj. Gen. Lehel writes, "As infantry has been unable to overcome the Zojila defences with the available artillery and air support, it was felt that the key to victory lay in the surprise use of tanks. It was absolutely vital to conceal the presence of tanks in the Zojila area. Tanks were moved from Jammu to Baltal at night with turrets removed and covered with tarpaulins to look like 3-ton vehicles. . .. The engineers under Major Thangaraju had converted the caravan route from Baltal to Zojila into a tankable road." (*The Indian Army: A Brief History*, pp. 78-79.) 20 October was fixed as the D-Day but due to inclement weather it had to be postponed and was finally fixed for midnight 31 October 1948. It was an agonising moment for our commanders. There had been heavy snow snowfall and our commanders wondered whether the tanks would slip or slide and get stuck in the slush.

Our commanders were deliberating whether to attack or not. Serbjeet Singh, maker of the documentary *Zojila* says about that decisive moment, 'Sparrow' broke the heavy silence, saying that while the weather had closed in making infantry movement difficult, he was quite willing to suffer the loss of even half his squadron . . . the attack must not be abandoned. His statement eased the tension and a new plan of attack was made. H-Hour was shifted from the midnight of 31 October to 10 a.m. on 1 November."

And then came the glorious moment, which military historians record and wonder over forever, and generations of officers talk about and savour. Gen. Thimmaya along with his commanders watched the dawn break on that glorious day. At 10.30 the leading tank No. BA 288009 called Chindwin, crossed the Zojila pass and fired its guns. The surprise was total. The Pakistanis were flabbergasted. Our Army radio operators picked up Pakistani wireless transmissions:

> "Sir, the Indians have got tanks on Zojila."
>
> "Tanks! Impossible. Tanks on Zojila! Don't be foolish."

"Sir, there are tanks !"

"Don't be stupid. I know those roads and the bridges. They are very weak. No tanks could have crossed those bridges. Impossible. Those bloody things are probably bloody jeeps made to look like tanks." (*Despatches From Kargil*, Srinjoy Chowdhury p. 29.)

The unexpected had happened. When the Pakistani Army's regulars, its irregulars, its tribal lascars and pathans saw the Indian tanks they lost their nerve and fled in panic. Our tanks took post after post. Drass was captured on 15 November. On 23 November 1948 our troops entered Kargil at 4 a.m.

It was the first time in the world that tanks were taken to such heights. Whenever we talk of Kargil, we should remember with gratitude the incomparable warrior Maj. Gen. K.S. Thimmaya, who would later rise to become India's Chief of Army Staff from 1957 to 1961 and his officers and jawans.

## The Jagged Tops of Kargil

Kargil was in danger once again in 1999. The Indian Army would battle once more to defend Kargil. Let us take a look at this 16,000-17000 feet high cruel mountain Kargil where in 1999 our soldiers and officers wrote with their blood, chapters of crimson glory.

During winter the temperature in Kargil plunges to -29 degrees Celsius. There is snowfall even in June on those ridges. Our soldiers climbed these snow-covered rocky slopes wearing clothes and shoes unsuitable for those heights, where one false step could make a person tumble down hundreds of feet and be broken into pieces, where the air is so short of oxygen that taking a few steps makes one breathless, where the icy winds seer the lungs and as if pierce through the bones, where the breath freezes under the nostrils to form icicles. In such extreme conditions our soldiers climbed up carrying a week's rations, arms and ammunition. While negotiating the steep rocks, sometimes, in order to lighten their burden and to be able to carry extra ammunition, they even threw away their chapattis and went without food for two or three days. To quench their thirst they sucked on pieces of snow, which due to the intense bombardment had become black from gunpowder. Yet our soldiers crushed all difficulties under their boots and kept advancing with courage, without fear, without turning their backs, even though from their positions of advantage on the heights, the Pakistanis rained bullets, bombs and boulders upon them.

Kargil consists of Mushkoh Valley, Drass, Kaksar and Batalik. This area is prone to avalanches and snow-storms. It is difficult to survive there during winter. Therefore, there was an unwritten agreement between India and Pakistan that during winter the contingents of both countries returned to the plains and during the summer went back to their respective positions and reoccupied their bunkers. In the winter of 1999, the Pakistanis broke this agreement and 2,000 Pakistanis advanced stealthily up to 4-8 kilometers inside the line of control and settled in our bunkers. They brought guns, mortars, anti-aircraft guns and other sophisticated arms. They also stocked up on choice foods like nuts, ghee etc.

The near-vertical slopes of those jagged snow-covered peaks, had to be scaled at night, in absolute silence, with fog reducing visibility, with hardly a toehold on the slippery rocks where our soldiers had to fix ropes with pitons and crampons. And if in the meantime, the enemy, who was holed up on the heights, saw them coming, there would be a rain of mortars, grenades, bullets and boulders upon them. Their buddies would fall dead by their side but there would be no time to linger or even to throw a backward glance at their dead fellow-soldiers lying on those snow-slopes with open, unseeing eyes. Nobody knew when, if ever, their bodies would be retrieved. At such moments a cold fury would possess the hearts of the surviving soldiers. They would advance with redoubled determination to annihilate the killers of their buddies, their brothers. They would get so primed up that they felt no pain and were not even aware of the bullets which pierced them, of the splinters which shredded their flesh, and of the blood which spouted from their wounds.

This war was fought on the heights, where due to lack of oxygen, breathing was difficult, where each step was an effort and one needed to stop to rest and recover after advancing every few steps, in temperatures of -29 to -32°C. In that killer cold, special clothing, shoes and goggles were required. There, apart from the Pakistanis, the greatest enemy of our soldiers was the merciless cold. Even the layers of thermal garments, special gloves and socks and insulated shoes could not stop the winds that pierced through these layers of clothing and froze their blood.

## Pakistan's Double Perfidy

The Kargil war was the third attempt by Pakistan to grab Kashmir from India. The Pakistanis deceived India and its army stealthily occupied the Kargil heights during the winter of 1999; the irony was that they encroached and entrenched themselves into bunkers built by the Indian Army.

Eternal vigilance is the requisite for guarding a country's freedom. But even after having fought three wars with Pakistan, we Indians were not wary; we were too easily deluded by Pakistan's show of good intentions. This time Pakistan played a charade in the full glare of cameras, watched by the world. With fanfare and girls dancing before his bus, India's prime minister, Atal Bihari Vajpayee, went to Lahore and signed a peace-pact with Pakistan's prime minister, Nawaz Sharif. It was noticed that the Chief of Pakistani Armed Forces, General Pervez Musharraf didn't attend the State dinner held in honour of the Indian Prime Minister. It is a moot point whether Nawaz Sharif knew that his army was preparing to infiltrate India. He claims that he was kept in the dark but the Pakistani Army says he was fully briefed. It is hard to believe that the army of a country can go to war without consulting its prime minister. Whatever the truth or falsehood of Nawaz Sharif's claim, we Indians cannot absolve ourselves for our lack of vigilance, especially against a devious and untrustworthy enemy.

Pakistan had meticulously planned and made preparations for this attack. The following episode is enough to prove it. In the -30°C temperature of Kargil, special clothes and boots are required. Indian soldiers did not have enough of these boots. In the entire world only one French firm makes this type of boots. When India tried to buy boots from the company they had no stock. On further enquiries, it was found that Pakistan had bought their entire stock in February 1999. (Vinayak Parab in *Salam Sainik* by Heeralal Yadav, pp. 26-27.)

## The War

For the Indian Army the situation was indeed difficult. Our soldiers did not have adequate shoes for climbing those rugged slopes; their rucksacks were too heavy to scale those heights carrying them. The Pakistanis entrenched on the tops shot with glee the Indian soldiers climbing up. Death danced around our soldiers. Even when their friends succumbed to enemy bullets and lay dead around them, our courageous jawans advanced without flinching, without fear of death, without a backward glance. Courage coursed through their hearts. It was as if they were competing to be the first to die for their country.

The soldiers of Pakistan's *Northern Light Infantry* were well-trained. They made their bunkers on the other slope of the mountain and covered their bunkers with iron sheets in such a way that it was very difficult for our guns to smash them. The Pakistanis had assumed that it would be impossible to dislodge them from the mountain ranges of Tololing, but by sacrificing their lives the brave hearts of the Indian Army's 2 Rajputana Rifles and 18 Grenadiers would achieve the impossible.

For the Indian Army the priority was to recapture the Tololing feature because from there the Pakistani gunners had at their mercy all the transport on National Highway 1 A. There had been fierce fighting and since 20 May the 18 Grenadiers had made three unsuccessful attempts to capture Tololing. On 2 June they launched a fourth attack. Advancing under fierce fire they crept up slowly and by 10 June had made a base only 30 meters below the Pakistani position.

"2 Rajputana Rifles used this firm base on 12 June to launch the assault on Tololing. The attack commenced at 11 p.m. and after fierce hand to hand fighting the Battalion secured Point 4590 by the early hours of 13 June. 18 Grenadiers now pushed through 2 Rajputana Rifles to secure a position three kilometers ahead of Point 4590. This position was then used for the attack on Point 5140, the highest feature in the Tololing complex. Two attempts by 13 Jammu & Kashmir Rifles met with limited success." (*The Indian Army: A Brief History*, Lieutenant General (Retd.) VK Singh, PVSM pp. 183-184-185.)

## Training in Ghumari: 6 June

Let us look at the epic battle through the eyes of Param Vir Sanjay Kumar. Sanjay recounts, "On 6 June 1999 our unit reached Ghumari. There for five days we were trained in mountain climbing. After a fierce battle for Tiger Hill on 12 June 1999, 13 Jammu & Kashmir was sent to help 2 Rajputana Rifles and 18 Grenadiers. Our battalion took charge from these two battalions. The commanding officer of our battalion was Lt. Colonel Y.K. Joshi. Major S.V. Bhaskar was the commander of 'A' Company, Captain S.S. Jamwal was the commander of 'B' Company, Major Gurpreet Singh commanded the 'C' Company and the commander of 'D' Company was Captain Vikram Batra. We were ordered to move to Drass as reserve to forces fighting at a feature called 'Hump', which was an extension of Tololing feature."

## Victorious battles for 'Hump', 'Rocky Knob' and 'Point 5140'

The Pakistanis had never shelled Drass before the Kargil War. Therefore no underground bunkers had been made to shelter civilians. Now that Drass had become an important front the civilian population had been evacuated.

Sanjay continues, " 'Hump' and 'Rocky Knob' were captured on 17 June 1999, after two nights of fierce fighting by 'A' and the 'C' Companies of 13 Jammu and Kashmir Rifles. Eight enemy soldiers were killed and nine were wounded. The Pakistani soldiers fled and left behind three universal machine guns (UMGs) which our officers and comrades used against the fleeing enemy soldiers.

"After the victory of 'Hump', 13 Jammu and Kashmir Rifles was asked to capture Point 5140, the highest peak on the Tololing Ridge, at an altitude of 17,000 feet. It was a strategic location on Tiger Hill. The enemy had brought down one of our helicopters from there. Unless it was captured no helicopter could land at Tololing Top. Therefore, it was of utmost importance to capture Point 5140. If it fell it would clear the Pakistanis from that sector and pave the way for a total Indian victory. The task was given to 'B' and 'D' Companies of 13 Jammu and Kashmir Rifles. On 19 June both companies moved quietly on the slopes of the 'Hump' and hid themselves. Both the Captains made a detailed reconnaissance of the snow-clad area. Our Battalion Commander, Lt. Colonel Y.K. Joshi briefed them in detail.

"Our 'B' and 'D' companies had only one night to finish our task because dawn lights up the mountain-tops earlier than the valley. Pakistani invaders had taken positions in bunkers at a height of 17,000 feet. From their vantage point, the enemy could see the advance of the Indian troops and target and kill them as they climbed the steep incline. When daylight faded from the mountain tops, 'B' and 'D' Companies began to move towards Point 5140 under cover of artillery fire. Aware of the enemy's advantage our Captain Vikram, decided to attack from the rear and thus take the Pakistanis by surprise. He ordered his men to climb the treacherous mountain stealthily. Each step was dangerous. Yet we crawled up silently. A wrong step could hurl a soldier down the mountain to certain death on the rocky ridge.

"It was tough to climb that 17,000-feet-high mountain in total darkness. We had to halt frequently to regain our breath. Time and again the area was illumined by the enemy artillery flares, which slowed us. The artillery fire of the enemy was dangerous for us. But unmindful of the risks we continued to advance towards Point 5140. The silence of those snow-clad hills was constantly broken by screaming bullets, the hellish din of guns, the aircraft wheeling above and the anti-aircraft artillery.

"That night we were so primed up that nothing or nobody could stop us. The anger inside us was exploding and the Pakistani soldiers kept on retreating from our fiery onslaught. We were not far from our target. At 3.15 a.m. the companies neared the feature, which had two bunkers on the top and five towards the east. 'B' Company under Captain S. S. Jamwal reached the top bunkers and attacked them. It was 3.25 a.m. The sun would rise at 4.30. We had only an hour to achieve the target.

"Captain Jamwal achieved his objective first and upon hearing his victory cry, "Oh Yeah, Yeah, Yeah", there was jubilation at the Command Headquarters. Inspired by our two young commanding Officers Captain Vikram and Jamwal, we attacked with renewed vigour. One after another our captains Vikram and Jamwal cleared 7 bunkers. In the fierce fighting eight Pakistani soldiers were killed and the others fled, many falling to their death from 16,900 feet. The 13 Jammu & Kashmir Rifles won a decisive victory. Not one of us was killed. Our troops captured a large quantity of arms, ammunition and even an anti-aircraft gun from those bunkers. Indian soldiers wrote a chapter of glory and held high the Tricolour on Point 5140. The Brigade Commander could not believe his ears when he was told that not a single soldier died in the operation. Chief of Army Staff, General Ved Prakash Malik, personally congratulated our Captain Vikram on the phone.

"From 19 June our Tricolour is flying on Point 5140."

With the capture of Point 5140 the tide of battle turned in the Drass Sector. Now helicopters could land at Tololing Top.

**Rest at Ghumari**

On 22 June 13 Jammu and Kashmir Rifles was again sent to Ghumari for rest and to look after their arms and replenish their ammunition. After about four days, their rest at Ghumari was cut short and on 30 June, 1999, 13 Jammu and Kashmir Rifles was sent for operations to win Point 4875 in the Mushkoh Valley under the command of 79 Mountain Brigade. All this was done in utmost silence and secrecy at night because from the top of Point 4875 the enemy could see them.

## Point 4875: The Last Battle

In May 1999 when our soldiers first attacked the stony plateau off Point 4875, compared to the enemy they were ill-clad and ill-equipped. The Pakistanis had them in sight of their guns and shot them at will. The worst part was that our soldiers were not acclimatised to fight on those heights. They succumbed to mountain sickness, due to which they suffered from disorientation, lack of capacity to fight and giddiness. The hurriedly set up hospitals did not have facilities to treat serious wounds and the wounded had to be carried by helicopter to hospitals far from the battlefields. But being a native of Himachal Pradesh young soldier Sanjay Kumar was no stranger to the snow covered peaks of the Himalayas.

This assignment was a near impossibility. It is difficult even to imagine the hellish conditions prevailing on those heights. But to win this point was absolutely necessary for India. From this point the Pakistani artillery had in its gun-sights the whole stretch of National Highway 1A from Drass to Matayan. On a stretch of 30-40 kilometers they could pick out any vehicle on the road. Many of our brave truck-drivers, who dared to travel on this stretch, were blasted by Pakistani artillery. Helicopters could not land at Drass as it was constantly targeted by the enemy. Even so our pilots flew their helicopters very low, along the Pandrass Ridge, but it was very risky.

On 1 July 1999, Lt. Colonel V. K. Joshi and the commander of 'A' Company, Major S. Vijay Bhaskar of 13 J&K Rifles climbed to a high vantage point to take a full view of the area of operation and draw up an attack plan. Based on their report the Commander prepared a battle plan at the headquarters of the 79 Mountain Brigade. On 2 July, Major General Mohinder Puri and Brigadier Kakkad discussed this plan. Now Sanjay's battalion was taken 1,500 meters below Point 4875 to an area which offered some cover where our troops of 17 Jat Regiment had made a fire base, under some overhanging rocks. On 2 and 3 July the soldiers of 13 J&K Rifles and 28 Rashtriya Rifles carried heavy weapons and ammunition for the battalion to this area.

On 4 July, the 'C' Company Commander Major Gurpreet Singh showed to the operation groups their objectives. He gave his last instructions. At 6 p.m. the Bofor guns commenced their bombardment.

## Victory at Point 4875 Flat Top

Rifleman Sanjay Kumar was the leading scout of the platoon advancing to attack Flat Top. Of that battle of battles, Sanjay recounts, "On 2 July 1999 our company was sent to Mushkoh Valley to chase the Pakistanis away from Point 4875 Flat Top. Our CO entrusted this task to our 'C' company. Major Gurpreet Singh was our company commander. He called the Company together and told us in detail about the coming battle. The climb was so difficult that youngest, lightest and fittest soldiers were selected for this attack. Mostly young officers and soldiers were martyred in this battle. I was in the scout group.

## 4 July

"The day for which we were waiting arrived. We gave our word to our CO that we would wager our lives to fulfill our objective. On the evening of 4 July 1999 our Company began climbing towards the fire base. 17 Jat Regiment had reached there before us. Ducking from the enemy shells we climbed up. It was a near vertical climb. There was little oxygen in the air and the higher we climbed the less became the oxygen. It was pitch dark. By the time we reached the fire base, day had dawned. We passed the whole day hidden under the rocks.

## 4 July: Night

"In the evening we began our advance. It was difficult enough to climb those snow-covered rocks, on top of it the heavy shelling by the enemy made our task more difficult. After a torturous climb during the night we reached the South-Spur. This spot was only 200 meters away from the enemy base. There were three peaks there, called Pimple 1 & Pimple 2 and Point 4875 Flat top. (The names of the different peaks in Kargil sector were given by staff officers without their corresponding to any physical feature of the concerned mountain peak. So these peaks did not resemble any pimple.)

"The enemy was watching us from Pimple 1. 17 Jat was to attack Pimple 1 and 'C' company of our 13 J&K Rifles was to annex Point 4875 Flat Top. The enemy began constant firing on us. Many of my comrades were wounded. The way was very narrow.

"As soon as we began to advance we came in the sights of the enemy guns. The enemy was familiar with that area and knew everything about the terrain. They somehow came to know that they were to be attacked at night and increased the firing. They used to increase the bombardment on the route we planned to take and also fired so much on the easier routes that we could not climb them and perforce had to take the more difficult routes. On the night of 5 July we could not reach our goal. The day dawned and the enemy began to fire upon us from both sides.

"Our Company Commander Major Gurpreet Singh talked with our CO Lt. Colonel Joshi and told him that we were being shelled from above and were dying. He asked for help. He told Lt. Colonel Joshi that if we received help in time we would attack and take our objective.

**5 July**

"Then on 5 July, Lt. Col. Joshi personally fired two Faggot Missiles from the fire-base. They were direct hits and we could see the enemy fleeing. From amongst our forward troops, one JCO and 10 soldiers including myself advanced under the screen of fire. Now whatever had to be done was to be done by 11 of us. With a loud cry of 'Durga Mata Ki Jai' we attacked the enemy. It was 10.30 a.m. Attack during day time is more difficult. We had to crawl on ice and move forward. If we stood up we would be felled by the enemy bullets. It was next to impossible to reach that difficult place and to engage the enemy. Since three days we have had no food. But we did not lose courage."

## Astounding Bravery: Stealing of Two Universal Machine Guns

When the sovereignty of a nation is threatened, when the outcome of a battle hangs in the balance, when the conditions seem dire, a moment comes when a simple village matriculate youth receives a daring impulse, straight from the guardian gods of Mother India. When darkness deepens and the Asura is poised to dominate the earth, when truth is about to be defeated by falsehood, when man the human is threatened by the demonic powers, then in those crucial moments come forward the gods and instil the spirit of unmatched bravery and unimaginable daring in a mortal heart. Something of Napolean's genius enters into a simple soldier. In such a moment a mortal becomes immortal and matches the gods in bravery. Did Kartikeya, the War God plant a gene of valour in Sanjay Kumar, the fourth recipient of Param Vir Chakra in Kargil War?

I do not think that manuals of war teach soldiers how to steal two UMGs, with barrels burning hot from constant shooting. Of that inspired moment of dare-devil courage and unparalleled daring, Sanjay writes, "Myself and one of my friends reached near a bunker of the enemy. At 16/17 thousand feet it was bitterly cold. Two universal machine guns were spewing deadly fire. These two UMGs became the greatest obstruction to our advance. I made a scheme with my friend. Each soldier is given two bandages which he can use for first aid in case he is wounded. I wrapped my bandages around my hands. Then at a sign from me, my friend threw a hand grenade inside that bunker. After it burst, for three or four seconds the wounded Pakistanis stopped firing the UMGs and I swooped like an eagle and with each hand holding the red hot muzzle of one UMG, lifted and dragged both of them out of the bunker."

Surely at that moment Sanjay Kumar became a lion of Durga. Some Divine Power had charged him with superhuman bravery. He says, "On that height of 16,000 feet the cold was so intense that holding those burning muzzles burnt the bandages on my hands but my palms were not burnt.

"In the seconds before they could react, I shot the three Pakistanis inside through the hole of the bunker with my AK 47 Rifle. Though the way to the bunker was from the back we made a way from the front and broke through and killed the rest of the enemy. Four of my comrades were wounded during this action. We carried them in the bunker and rendered first aid to them.

"Generally the first bunker is the strongest and it has the most men and arms. If it is captured, it is easier to conquer the other bunkers because usually they have only light machine guns and 3 or 4 soldiers. The enemy had collected lots of arms and ammunition in that first bunker. We picked up their UMG and began to fire at the second bunker. We planned that only six jawans including me, would attack the next bunker and the others would help us by firing from the first bunker so that we could reach the second bunker easily. But the enemy guessed our scheme. They silently hid one soldier to the left of the bunker. We did not see him. We were advancing in groups of twos when that hidden Pakistani began to shoot. In a moment two of my friends were martyred. The rest of us four were also wounded. The enemy started such a barrage of bullets that for 15 minutes we were unable to move. I was hit by several bullets, one in my left leg and another in my hip. But I had no time or first aid material to bandage my wounds. My bandages had been burnt when I lifted the two UMGs.

"My friends were more wounded than me. The wound in my leg was serious. Blood flowing out of this wound was filling my gumboot. But due to the intense cold the pain was muffled. Therefore I did not look at my wounds. My comrades had taken two or even three bullets at one place. I began to look after their wounds.

"After some time the barrage of bullets stopped. We saw that the enemy soldiers were going leisurely towards their upper bunker. They thought that after such intense shelling none of the Indians would be alive. But four of us were alive. When I saw them climbing up I lifted their UMG and let off a rain of bullets which killed them. Upon seeing this, the enemy soldiers holed up in the upper bunker ran away. We began to climb up.

"We climbed with great difficulty. Because of our wounds it was doubly difficult to climb those snow and sleet covered slippery rocks. We fired while we crawled and thus reached the next bunker. We threw hand grenades inside the bunker but there was no movement inside. Then we peeped through the hole. There was nobody there. We entered and took over the bunker. Then I glanced down and saw two enemy soldiers running down. I set the UMG on the other side of the bunker and killed those two soldiers.

"By now the firing from behind had stopped. And many other jawans of our company had reached there. We had killed fifteen enemy soldiers. Lots of weapons, ammunition and rations fell into our hands. We were glad that we had fulfilled the work entrusted to us but our joy was marred by the fact that two of our comrades had died. It was 5 a.m. We put the Tricolour of India on Flat Top.

"The victory at Flat top opened the way for the victory of Point 4875 by a unit of 13 J&K Rifles under the command of Captain Vikram Batra. He chased away the enemy though he was martyred in this battle. And thus the National Highway from Drass to Matayan was once more free of the menace of Pakistani shelling.

"The Company doctor gave us first aid and arranged to send us down. That night we reached our fire-base and after that reached the nalla from where vehicles took us to Ghumari. At Ghumari our wounds were treated. On 6 July helicopters took us to Srinagar. After passing four days in Srinagar we were taken to Chandigarh hospital. After five days' treatment in Chandigarh I was sent to Lucknow command hospital. My wounds were healing quickly; therefore I was discharged after 15 days and came home on 45 days' leave.

## Victory

"The exultation of victory was marred by sorrow because we had lost three officers and dozens of soldiers. The death of most Indian soldiers was caused by the anti-aircraft guns and universal machine guns (UMGs) of the Pakistanis. They had large quantities of high quality mortars, machine guns, rocket launchers, grenade launchers,

Kalashnikov rifles, night-vision glasses and heaps of ammunition. They had also stored large quantities of ghee and dry fruits. After the victory, apart from the arms and ammunition our troops also found in the bunkers the personal effects, letters and diaries, medals and identity cards, family photographs etc. of slain Pakistani officers and soldiers. The credit for the victory of Three Pimples goes to martyrs like Lieutenant Vijayant Thapar, Major Padmapani Acharya and other officers and soldiers who laid down their life on those icy slopes."

We had blundered in trusting the Pakistanis and had to pay a great price for our mistake. "In this war India's casualities were 519, wounded 1365 and missing one. Pakistani casualties are estimated to be 737 killed including some 71 officers." (*The Indian Army: A Brief History*, Lieutenant General (Retd.) VK Singh, PVSM p.188.)

These vainglorious Pakistanis never expected that the Indian brave hearts would pulverise their pride under their boots and shatter their dreams of annexing Kargil and Kashmir. God always helps those who are on the side of Truth. God filled our officers and soldiers with the power of Durga and the determination to make the supreme sacrifice for the country. There was as if a competition as to who would sacrifice his life first. Again and again our officers and soldiers walked into the jaws of death. They knew that there was little possibility of their returning alive but "To win or to die" was their pledge.

## The Golden Tale of Bravery on the High Tops of Kargil

Pakistanis used to brag that each Pakistani soldier was equal to ten Indian soldiers. In the three wars with India, in 1947, 1965 and 1971 the pride of Pakistan lay pulverised in the dust. The rest of their delusions died an ignominious death in Kargil. They were to realise that each Indian soldier was more potent than four Pakistani soldiers. Actually, the pride of Pakistan had died a natural death the day General Niazi and more than 93,000 fully armed soldiers had made a most abject surrender before the Indian Army. Those who surrendered were the cruel cowards who had killed three million civilians of East Bengal with utmost barbarity.

On 7 July 1999 our troops conquered Point 4875. Faced with a total defeat, in desperation, Pakistan began to make overtures for a ceasefire. Their dreams of victory and of avenging the defeat at Siachen lay in the dust. On 4 July itself, even before Point 4875 was conquered, Nawaz Sharif hurried to Washington and requested President Bill Clinton to broker a ceasefire. Pakistan announced a unilateral withdrawal of its troops from Indian soil.

## The Winning of Param Vir Chakra

Sanjay continues his narration, "While I had still some days' leave left, a man of my village brought a newspaper and said, 'Sanjay you have made the whole country and our village proud of you. Look, your photograph and the tale of your bravery have been printed in the newspaper.' At the same time a major of my unit along with a JCO and a jawan reached my home and took me with them. I could not believe that I had won the greatest honour of the Indian Army. I had joined the Army only three years back. I thought that the Param Vir Chakra is given to those who have died and I was getting it while being still alive. I considered myself most lucky. One cannot guess the happiness of my family. They were proud that their beloved son had brought honour to the family.

"On 26 January 2000 the President of India gave me the Param Vir Chakra."

## Citation

### Rifleman Sanjay Kumar

### 13 Jammu and Kashmir Rifles (13760533)

Rifleman Sanjay Kumar volunteered to be the leading scout of the attacking column tasked to capture area Flat Top of Point 4875 in the Mushkoh valley on 4 July 1999. During the attack when enemy automatic fire from one of the sangars posed stiff opposition and stalled the column, Rifleman Sanjay Kumar realising the gravity of the situation and with utter disregard to his personal safety, charged at the enemy. In the ensuing hand-to-hand combat, he killed three of the intruders and was himself seriously injured. Despite his injuries, he charged onto the second sangar. Taken totally by surprise, the enemy left behind a Universal Machine Gun and started running.

Rifleman Sanjay Kumar picked up the UMG and killed the fleeing enemy. Although bleeding profusely, he refused to be evacuated. The brave action on his part motivated his comrades and they took no notice of the treacherous terrain and charged onto the enemy and wrested the area Flat Top from the hands of the enemy.

Rifleman Sanjay Kumar displayed most conspicuous gallantry, cool courage and devotion to duty of an exceptionally high order in the face of the enemy.

Gazette of India Notification

No. 16 – Press/2000

*Being Awarded PVC by the President*

## The Pride of the Indian Army: 13 Jammu and Kashmir Rifles

As mentioned before, Sanjay intensely aspired to join 13 Jammu & Kashmir Rifles, the battalion to which his martyred uncle had belonged. By God's Grace Sanjay was posted to his uncle's battalion.

13 Jammu & Kashmir Rifles is the pride of the Indian Army. It happened for the first time in the history of Indian Army that in one battle of one war, in the same action two warriors of the same battalion were awarded the highest battle-honour of India, the Param Vir Chakra. Of these two, Captain Vikram Batra offered his life at the altar of Mother India and won this award, and the other, the hero of this story, Sanjay Kumar defeated both the enemy and death to win this honour. Generally, soldiers are honoured to be a part of an illustrious battalion but PVCs Vikram Batra and Sanjay Kumar added luster to the name of their battalion.

## Most Humble

It is difficult to find a man so unassuming and humble as PVC Sanjay Kumar. Of average height and build, when one looks at this quiet man for a moment one doubts that he could have pulled out and carried away two blazing UMGs, picking them up by their red hot nozzles. From his appearance one cannot guess that this young man is a blazing fire of daring and bravery. When awarded the Param Vir Chakra, he said, "I give all the credit for this to my unit and my company. The credit for this award goes equally to the co-operation and self-sacrifice of my comrades. I did not do anything alone. Whatever was done was achieved by all of us together. Maybe other soldiers showed greater bravery than me but in the eyes of our commanders the dragging out of the UMGs was an act of supreme bravery. I followed the order of my commander and did what was expected of me to the best of my ability. It was the battle plans of our commanders and the encouragement they gave us which led us to victory."

## The Feelings of Soldiers during Battle

About the feelings of soldiers during battle Sanjay says, "When we attack, our attention is focused totally on our aim. Leave aside our family members, we do not even think of those in front or behind. Only when we rest, we remember our families. Our letters are brought to the very battlefield. The porters who bring ammunition for us also bring our letters. But if the battle is prolonged, for days nothing reaches us. When it seemed likely that the battle would last for several days then we were asked to carry food with us. In such situations we carried some roasted gram and jaggery and when thirsty we would suck pieces of snow which had turned black due to the shelling. We used to joke that if we did not die of shelling we will die sucking this contaminated snow. By the time we conquered our objective our ammunition would be exhausted, and then we used the ammunition left behind by the enemy. In this war we found lots of arms and ammunition left behind by the enemy.

"During the war the victory of the leading unit makes the work of the following troops easier. The difficult thing was that we had to fight while climbing because the enemy was already entrenched on the top. The ascent was so hair raising that in the morning when we peeped from above, we used to wonder how we could have managed to climb this impossible-seeming route. At night we marched together. The enemy unleashed a barrage of shells every five minutes. When they fired flares, we lay flat on the ground. In the light of the flares we would also see the terrain and decide which route we had to take. During the day we prepared a base under rocks from where the enemy could not spot us but the shells of our big guns could strike at them and could cover us when we marched.

"A path went upwards from Mushkoh Nala. If you look down from Flat Top then you can see clearly the village of Drass and the National Highway to Leh. The enemy was holed up on Flat Top. They could see our climbing troops and informed their guns about our positions and then they rained shells upon us. In this battle being fought at 15,000-16,000 feet more than a dozen of our soldiers died and 60/70 of them were wounded.

### At Present

"After receiving the Param Vir Chakra I married my betrothed Pramila. On 21 August 2001, we had a son whom we named Neeraj Thakur. On 17 January 2005, our daughter was born, whom we have named Muskan Thakur. I am working happily in my unit of 13 J&K Rifles.

### Prizes

"At first for winning the Param Vir Chakra the Central Government gave as reward Rs. 1,500 per month which has been increased to Rs. 10,000. Himachal Government gave me a reward of Rs. 1,75,000/-. The State Government used to give a monthly stipend of Rs.4,500/-, now it has been increased to Rs. 125,000/- yearly. In the military if a soldier dies, until his service period is finished, his family gets his full salary. After the service period is over, the family gets a pension."

### The Remarkable Bond Between Indian Officers and Soldiers

The credit for the Indian victory also goes to the intimate relations and feeling of brotherhood between Indian Army officers and soldiers. The officers of the Indian Army take great care of their jawans. They stand and fight shoulder to shoulder with them and lead from the front. In proportion to soldiers, more Indian Army officers sacrifice their life than in any other Army of the world. On the other hand there is a great gulf between the Pakistani officers and soldiers. The Pakistani officers think it is below their dignity to mix with the soldiers and to treat them as equals. They send their soldiers in the front to fight and die and themselves fight from behind.

## 26 July: Kargil Victory Day

Today India celebrates 26 July as Kargil victory day. On that day we should offer our homage to the brave hearts of the Indian army who sacrificed their lives, lost their limbs and won Kargil for India. The task was so difficult that Army officers all over the world watched it with great interest to see how the Indians would achieve the nearly impossible. Few believed that India would come out victorious from this trial. But by their bravery and courage the Indian Armed Forces' highly trained officers, non-commissioned officers, junior-commissioned officers and soldiers made possible the impossible. They won victory as if it was an easy task. We should remember and felicitate them and should etch their tales on our hearts. We have been defeated by invaders since centuries. India's victory during the fourteen days' Bangladesh War in 1971 and the victory at Kargil in 1999 have washed off the millennial black mark of defeat.

But we should be alert to see that Kargil is not repeated. We should watch every inch of our Motherland.

*Being facilitated at a function by COAS*

## Lightning of God

Like a bullet,
Fine-tuned and primed
When its target is fixed
And by destiny decided,
None can stop from striking
Indra's bolt of lightning.

When screeching shells
Rained fire, shrapnel and death spilt,
When flares lighted the midnight
Exposing all who stood or ran,
Onward our Indian soldiers marched
Torn by hunger and thirst,
Through gun-powder blackened snow.
As they marched, as they climbed,
Constantly from the heights
The enemy rained bullets
Which easily found their aim,
Piercing and shredding their limbs.
Yet, on sheer and slippery rocks
Ascended the Indian soldiers,
Their hearts flaming with rage;
They crouched, sprang forward
And rose undaunted.

That day, when two Pakistani
Machine guns spewed death,
Kartikeya, the warrior God,
Entered the heart of a mortal.
As a tiger crouches and springs,

And snatches its prey,
Rifleman Sanjay snatched
Those guns, one in each hand,
Holding their red-hot nozzles.
Dodging the exploding shells,
Sanjay, soldier of the army of Gods
Silenced those guns,
Those messangers of death.
Thus was won the battle
Thus was conquered
Point 4875 at Kargil.

**Kali Appeased**

"Blood! Rivers of blood!
Thirsty I am for the oblation of
Indian brave hearts' blood –
This only will I accept
In lieu of victory
In exchange for freedom."

Thus cried and danced
Naked Kali, Goddess fierce
Thirsty for the lives of warriors
On the peaks of Kargil.

For, too long if peace reigns,
Nations lose their will
And their right to be,
Men lose their manliness.
In the sacred Yajna of freedom
War is the ritual pot, in which,

At their country's altar,
The sentinels of the frontier
Their lives willingly offer.
Like incense burns
Like Roman candles burst
And shower on the sacred motherland
Crimson flowers of blood
The sacred bodies of martyrs.

Behold! Kali was appeased at Kargil
By our Indian heroes' willing immolation.

# Author

Shyam Kumari was born in Muzaffarnagar, U.P., in 1934. There she studied in the Vedic Putri Pathshala and S. D. Degree College up to her B.A. In 1965, she passed her M.A. from Lucknow University. She has read widely in Hindi and English literature, as well as religious and spiritual books.

Since her childhood she yearned to find God. In 1969, the Divine Mother accepted her in Sri Aurobindo Ashram and appointed her a teacher in the Sri Aurobindo International Centre of Education.

Hundreds of her poems, lyrics, stories, plays, literary and social essays, both in English and Hindi, have appeared in national and international journals. She has also written and published more than 70 books, some running into several reprints. Many of her books have been translated into Hindi, Oriya, Tamil, Bengali, Marathi and Gujarati. She has written path-breaking rhymes and story books for children. In 1998 she launched a Hindi quarterly magazine, Swarna Hansa which she, single-handedly, wrote, edited and published for 20 years.

In 1998, she established Vraja Trust, a public charitable trust, and is at present its managing trustee. In 2001, she started *Sri Aravinda Sanskrit Vidyalaya,* in Pondicherry, India, to impart free Sanskrit education to children and adults alike and she is its Chairperson. In 2005, she launched the "Let Each School Adopt a Hero" scheme. In 2006, she launched the "Let Us Honour Our Soldiers" and "Let each child become a Hero Warrior" schemes.

www.ingramcontent.com/pod-product-compliance
Lightning Source LLC
LaVergne TN
LVHW090518110826
845146LV00003B/901

* 9 7 8 9 3 9 0 4 3 9 7 8 2 *